The Boy from Berlin

Two victims of the Holocaust

R.M. Burt

"Thomas und seine Mutti", February 1938.

THE BOY FROM BERLIN

TWO VICTIMS OF THE HOLOCAUST

The story of Tom Walters told by

R M BURT

Silver Fish
publishing

British Library Cataloguing in Publication Data
A record for this book is available from the British Library

ISBN 1 902134 13 3

Printed and bound in Great Britain by
Cox & Wyman, Reading, Berks

Silver Fish Publishing is a division of
Silver Fish Creative Marketing Ltd
37 Pottery Lane, Holland Park
London W11 4LY

Contents

Acknowledgements

In writing this account of Tom Walters' life, help is gratefully acknowledged from members of his family and from many friends:

Dan Bowman, Alan Jones, Susan Koenigsberg (letters and papers, including many written by the late Hanna Baumann, sister of Tom's mother).

Mrs Boulton, Jim Ross, Larry Dowden, John Wood (interviews about Tom, Mr Archie Boulton and wartime Birkenhead).

Annelies Marshall, Sidney Morris, Marion Rushton (advice on German national anthem and on Judaism; checking German and English text).

Arthur Pallett (technical assistance with computer and scanner).

Jim Wilkinson (interview about the Hollybush Fellowship).

George Lihou (interview about the Jonas Trust).

Regine Wosnitza (invaluable research; Regine deserves the highest praise for professional efficiency, imagination and human sympathy. Without her willing contribution, this book could not have been written).

Foreword

A smiling face and an outstretched hand coming towards me, coupled with the words "Hello, I'm Tom" was my first introduction to the man who is the principal subject of this book. That was over a decade ago and I have come to the realisation down the years that my first impression, from that short statement, was a true one: here was a man of security, clarity and vision. His life-story has unfolded to me piece by piece over the years, but has been enlarged and expanded dramatically since a documentary T.V. programme was produced about his life, which involved detailed research at that time.

Tom has not arrived where he is today by chance, but through humility, perseverance, and a contagious work ethic; surrounded by his foster family who became his adoptive parents, a caring church family and a Christian wife. The fact that he has not only survived, but succeeded from being a tender shoot, torn away from his childhood surroundings, transplanted, to put down deep roots and grow into a strong tree in the land of his adoption, is a miracle.

As the story unfolds, the character of the man is moulded. His influence and dedication built up a formidable workforce, especially when declaring, "I won't ask anyone to do what I am not willing to do myself". His fervent love and commitment to his Lord and Saviour giving him strength and guidance, and a caring wife and family spurring him on with support, are ample testimony to this gentle spirited man who will one day meet his Master and say, "Hello, I'm Tom", and the reply will be, "I know, come on in". May this book lead you to the same holy familiarity.

Jim Wilkinson,
Hollybush Fellowship,
Newsham, Thirsk, YO7 4DH

Chapter 1

Bombs in Birkenhead

War is a terrible thing. It has often been said that no-one ever wins a war. Everyone loses. The question is whether it can ever be the lesser of two evils. How much destruction and death are the price worth paying to get rid of a tyrant?

One of the new features of the 1939-45 war was the involvement of the whole population, especially those who lived in cities. True, the whole population was involved in the 1914-18 war, in that day after day and week after week came the news of appalling slaughter as the flower of Britain's youth perished in their thousands with unimaginable suffering, for a cause that no-one seemed to understand; but for most people, the war itself, the death and destruction, were far away, in France or beyond. In the second world war it was different, because of the new potential for aerial bombardment and because Hitler's fanatical and ruthless ambitions were of a different order and on a different scale from those of first world war Germany.

For the first few phoney months, uninformed jingoistic optimists talked of the war being over by Christmas, just as they had on both sides in 1914, when the Kaiser boasted that he would eat his Christmas dinner in Buckingham Palace! Incidentally, he was still alive in 1939, and died peacefully in occupied Holland in 1941.

With such a short interval between the two wars, there were many whose memories of the first filled them with anxiety as the second conflict began. The old euphoria had disappeared. Another change from the first world war days was that almost every home in Britain could listen to the wireless, to the exhortations of the Prime Minister, not to mention, as time went on, the propaganda of "Lord Haw-haw" (William Joyce), aimed at intimidating the British public with his scorn and threatening references to particular towns, including some in the Wirral peninsula, which he knew. The news bulletins and calls to patriotism were listened to in homes throughout the land. One of the calls to support the war effort was for all the iron railings and gates in front of people's houses to be ripped out and taken away to make armaments. Was all this metal really useful for making guns, or was it simply a scheme to raise the nation's morale?

Thousands of schoolchildren were evacuated from the cities and boarded with families in rural areas, but many of them were brought back before anything happened, because families felt the strain of living apart. They would stay in the cities and hope for the best. But there were some, more politically aware, who expected the worst. They knew that the threat of German aggression this time carried with it the sinister policies of Hitler's Nazi régime, with its philosophy of a master race, a thousand-year Reich, and the extermination of anyone or anything that stood in the way. They knew of Hitler's determination to overturn the humiliation suffered by Germany under the terms of the Treaty of Versailles in 1919; and his determination, at the same time, to get rid of the economic burden caused by massive claims for compensation by the victorious powers. By means of a huge programme of re-armament, he had virtually wiped out the 30% unemployment of the 1930s. In 1933 he took total powers, banned trade unions, announced the building of 2,500 miles of *Autobahn*, proudly displayed the new "people's car" (*Volkswagen*), gave help to farmers; and the State radio proclaimed the greatness of the German nation. At the same time, he saw an opportunity to exploit old hatreds and jealousies by blaming all the country's problems on a scapegoat: the Jews. He denounced Jewish writers, lawyers, scientists, doctors; and in April 1933 he authorised Goebbels to order a nation-wide boycott of Jewish businesses. Jews were expelled from their careers in medicine, law and the civil service. Marriage between Jewish and non-Jewish Germans became a criminal offence. Jewish children were expelled from the State schools and other children were taught in school how to identify Jews and to be on their guard against them. Incidentally the gypsies suffered a similar fate under the Nazi genetic theories of a pure Aryan race, but their fate has attracted less notice, because they were fewer in number and far less likely to have professional status.

In March 1938, Austria was absorbed into the German Reich, in violation of the 1919 peace settlement, which Hitler treated with contempt. The Austrians as a whole welcomed the move, for there were long-standing fascist tendencies in Austria. It was also a country noted for anti-Semitic attitudes. In a recent novel, *The Vienna Passage*, David Porter paints a picture of the early twentieth century in that city, when even some respected leaders of Christian churches thought it right to attack the Jews. At that time, Vienna had a large and prosperous Jewish population. It also had among its temporary residents the young Adolf Hitler, who, as an 18-year-old would-be student, took the entrance examination to the Vienna Academy of Arts — and failed. He was furiously humiliated by this insult, as he saw it; and spent the next few months in a wilderness of aimless resentment. Some have maintained that during this period he contracted syphilis from a Jewish prostitute. Certainly he imbibed the anti-Semitic invective of the ex-priest Lanz von Liebenfels, together with his use of the swastika as a fascist symbol. Thirty years later his ferocious jealousy of the Jews was expressed through brutal laws of discrimination. In 1938 Jews were harassed and persecuted throughout the Reich; humiliated by being ordered to scrub the streets, while people stood and laughed. In Munich a synagogue was pulled down on the pretext that it was a traffic hazard. And then came *Kristallnacht* (the night of the 9th/10th November 1938), when a thousand synagogues were burned, three hundred Jews killed and 30,000 Jews rounded up. One hundred thousand managed to emigrate in 1938 and 1939, although some countries were reluctant to accept them. Switzerland soon became well-known for sending back "illegal" refugees. In addition, those who escaped to France, Poland, Holland or Belgium, soon faced the same trauma all over again as the German invasions continued.

It was the German troops marching into Czechoslovakia and then Poland that brought Britain to a declaration of war. Then came the shock of the rapid invasion of Holland, Belgium and Norway, and the devastating news in June 1940 that France had capitulated. From then on England was within easy reach of the enemy's shells and bombs. The south coast was pounded and the cities mercilessly attacked — London, Birmingham, Bristol, Coventry, Sheffield, Hull, Liverpool and Merseyside. And it is in Merseyside that our story continues.

Between Liverpool and North Wales lies the Wirral peninsula, separated from Wales by the River Dee and from Liverpool and south Lancashire by the River Mersey — hence the name Merseyside which is sometimes applied to this area. Opposite Liverpool, on the Wirral side, is the town of Birkenhead; and next to Birkenhead, a little further inland, the dormitory town of Bebington. Liverpool was one of Britain's leading ports at the beginning of the war, with seven miles of docks; and Birkenhead, on the other side of the river, was equally important for its shipbuilding at Cammell Laird's. Nearly all the submarines needed in the war were built here (with the remainder at Vickers, Barrow-in-Furness). Since the average survival time of a submarine was about six months, the industry was of the utmost urgency. It also made Birkenhead a prime target for enemy attack. A former resident remembers, as a six-year-old boy, being able to see the huge cranes of the shipyard from his bedroom window. He also remembers being snatched up from under the stairs where they were hiding, and carried by his mother, when the house received a direct hit in May 1941. His father worked on the railway, which was also a prime target. As for the submarines, there was one dramatic disaster even before the war, when the "Thetis" was out on its maiden sea-trials in Liverpool Bay in 1939. Something went wrong with one of the valves, and then with the escape apparatus, and about a hundred men on board died of suffocation. The submarine was pulled out of the shallow water onto the shores of Anglesey and towed to Holyhead; then later taken back to Cammell Laird's at Birkenhead, where it was re-equipped and renamed the "Thunderbolt", surviving until 1943, when it was sunk with all hands near Cape San Vito, on the west coast of Sicily. The full story of the original disaster (the worst submarine disaster ever) is told in *Thetis, 'The Admiralty Regrets'*, by Warren and Benson (Avid Publications), who include the information that at the time (June 1939) King George VI received a telegram of sympathy from the German Chancellor, Adolf Hitler!

Every war produces a catalogue of casualties, from spectacular acts of mass destruction, which shock the world at first, but quickly settle down into more impersonal statistics of how many were killed or wounded; to less conspicuous but moving tales of individual heroism and suffering. Sometimes the emphasis is on the suffering: the pain and fear of the moment, the long-term emotional disorder, damaged career prospects and broken families. At other times, and especially during the conflict, all attention is on the heroism, the courage of those who fight for their country, even "our glorious dead" who made the supreme sacrifice in the fight against an evil empire.

The *Birkenhead News* of 1941 reflects this complexity of emotions. On the 28th May it carried the headline, "Birkenhead helps to sink Bismarck" and continued, "The great battleship, Prince of Wales, which was built at Cammell Laird's, took part in the engagement that sent Germany's newest and most powerful battleship to the bottom". Planes from the aircraft carrier Ark Royal also took part in the attack — seen as avenging the sinking of HMS Hood earlier in the year. On the 2nd November the German News Agency reported that the port of Birkenhead had been attacked by the Luftwaffe. High explosives and incendiary bombs were dropped at Birkenhead by a "strong formation" of bombers and "in good visibility numerous hits and fires were observed in the Mersey area". During this same week, on the 8th November, there is a report that three conscientious objectors, one of them a spiritualist medium, had been sent to prison for refusing to join the armed forces. Then on the 15th November came the news that the Ark Royal had been sunk; and on the 29th another of her few survivors had struggled home to Birkenhead, where the ship had been built. And on the 13th December (six days after the Japanese attack on Pearl Harbour), news of further disaster, presented in terms of tragic glory: "Prince of Wales goes down fighting. Birkenhead mourns mighty battleship. Short but historic career. With her guns blazing, proud and defiant... attacked by sixty Japanese planes".

The whole Merseyside area was attacked with devastating ferocity from 1940 to 1942. On both sides of the Mersey the raids were so heavy and so frequent that it is a wonder the cities of Liverpool and Birkenhead survived to tell the tale. Statistics given in the *Birkenhead News* tell us that in these two cities and Wallasey (also on the Mersey), 10,000 houses were destroyed. In Bootle (part of Liverpool), 16,000 of its 17,000 houses were damaged. In Birkenhead there were 35,727 houses in 1939; 2,079 were destroyed and 26,000 damaged. No-one living in the area at that time will ever forget the raids of May 3rd to 7th 1941: five nights with five raids, which the Germans' own news described as their "heaviest ever". On May 3rd, there were direct hits on the Liverpool museum, a technical college, a theatre, the public library, Lewis's and other stores, the customs house, the docks, as well as countless private houses and businesses. 66,000 incendiary bombs fell on the city during the night of May 4th. The "Royal Daffodil" ferry boat, built at Cammell Laird's in 1934, was destroyed in the river on the 8th May at 10 p.m., when a bomb apparently went straight through it and exploded in the mud beneath. Similar destruction, including the Argyle Theatre, took place on the Birkenhead side, where there had already been severe damage in the city centre from as early as August 1940. On the 14th May 1941, a thousand corpses were brought to the cemetery at Anfield (Liverpool) and buried in a common grave. And throughout it all, "ordinary" life went on, albeit coloured and directed by the ramifications of the war; for instance, the *Bebington News* reports that on the 6th June 1942 King Haakon of Norway (whose country was under German occupation), visited Bebington and stayed with Lord and Lady Leverhume at Thornton Manor.

It was at Bebington that the Walters family lived, at No. 46 Town Lane. The family consisted of a middle-aged couple, Chris and Eva Walters, their nine-year-old son Tom, and Eva's mother, who had been bombed out of her home in Mossley Hill, Liverpool. The premises were a corner shop, which was run by Eva, while Chris supported with an ironmongery round. Always a friendly and hospitable couple, they were well known and trusted in the neighbourhood.

Tom vividly describes the unforgettable night when their house received a direct hit from an incendiary bomb, crashing through the upstairs into the shop below. Chris was out on patrol duty as an ARP warden. The others were sheltering under the stairs, but quickly escaped into the street, climbing over rubble and between the burning shattered gas mains. Now they were homeless. They knocked on doors, asking for shelter. None of the other houses was hit, although most of them had windows blown out by the blast. A neighbour (one of their customers) took them in for a couple of nights — even the evil of the blitz produced some good, in the way it drew people together and often showed them at their best, coming to each other's rescue and willing to share their meagre resources and cramped accommodation. Then a temporary home was found for them by Mr A.H. Boulton, a leading Bebington builder and an elder in the Brethren church known as "Bethesda". He offered them a two-roomed sales office shed on a building site, and here they stayed for quite a while, while affairs were sorted out.

Mr Archie Boulton was well known in Bebington, which is not surprising because he built most of it. He started work in his father's building firm as a school leaver at the end of the nineteenth century, but he was too independent and ambitious to be content with that, and by the time he reached his late teens had set up a firm of his own. He built his first house in Birkenhead, although the bank refused him a loan. His firm went from strength to strength. Perhaps he should be in the Guinness Book of Records for length of career as head of his own building firm, for he died in 1986 at the age of 102. A possible rival for the record would be his friend Sir John Laing, who had an even more spectacular career and died at a similar age. Mr Boulton built in Prenton and Heswall as well as Bebington; and it was not only houses that he built, though unlike Sir John he would not build a public house or a wine shop.

How then did the Walters family come to know Mr Boulton? Not, in the first instance, as a builder, but as a "brother", for they were members of the same church. It was Mr Boulton who built the church. That is to say, he designed and put up the building. But even if we say, as he would most certainly have done, that the church is the people, not the building, he would still be recognised as one of its builders. For this kind of building was every bit as important to him as the other. What then was so important about this church?

Tom aged nine, Bebington, 1941.

Bethesda Church, Bebington.

Mr Archie Boulton (right), with evangelist
and Bible teacher Mr Harold St John.

The shop run by Chris and Eva Walters, until they were bombed
out in 1942.

Chapter 2

Brethren background

There have always been two opposing tendencies in the Church: those who want to set up a hierarchy of leaders, with titles and pomp and ceremony; and those who emphasise simplicity and equality, with as few labels as possible.

Every now and then a new movement sets itself the task of getting rid of dead traditions and giving central place once more to the teaching and practice of the Church in New Testament times. Quite often the members of such a movement decline to give themselves a name (which they see as part of the dead tradition), because they want to regain the unity of the early Church rather than simply add one more to the multiplicity of denominations. One result of this studied anonymity may be that "their" churches never become well known in the world generally, or if they do attract publicity (good or bad), they run the risk of being landed with a nick-name.

E.H. Broadbent, in his book, *The Pilgrim Church*, gives a fascinating account of the existence and activities of such groups from the earliest centuries to the present time. In the time of Constantine, and long afterwards, they were often known as Cathars (meaning "pure living"). In later centuries there were the Bogomils ("friends of God") in Bosnia, the Waldensians and Albigenses in France and

Italy, as well as better known (though often misunderstood) groups such as the Hussites, Mennonites, Anabaptists and Huguenots. One group of German colonists in Russia in the early nineteenth century simply called their meetings "Stunden", meaning "hours". They called each other brethren, but their critics gave them the name Stundists. At that time there was considerable freedom in Russia; indeed it is interesting to note that in the year that Napoleon invaded Russia (1812), the Czar Alexander I was encouraging the establishment in his country of a branch of the British and Foreign Bible Society. By the end of the century, however, this had changed. A decree issued in 1893 ordered that the children of Stundists were to be taken away from their parents, whose names would be posted up in public places, so that they would not be able to find employment — a tactic already used in seventeenth-century France against the Huguenots, and to be used on a fearful scale in the twentieth century against the Jews in all the countries under Hitler's control.

About the same time as the appearance of the "Stundists" in Russia, other similar movements were springing up elsewhere, often independently and then discovering each other later. One group, beginning in Scotland, Ireland and the United States, became known as the "Churches of Christ". They are still found here and there in the United Kingdom, and in large numbers in the USA and Australia. Another meeting began in Dublin in the 1820s, under the leadership of Anthony Norris Groves, John Vesey Parnell, John Nelson Darby, and others. Groves was a dentist, who later went to Baghdad and India as a missionary. Parnell was afterwards Lord Congleton; and Darby was a Church of England clergyman, godson of Lord Nelson — hence his middle name. The aim of all these groups was to get back to the New Testament. What did that mean? Basically, four things: acceptance of the Bible as final authority; an independent local congregation; baptism of believers only, therefore no baptism of infants; and rejection of "denominations", with all true believers, from any denomination, welcome to share communion.

The Dublin group flourished and spread to Bristol, largely under the leadership of George Müller, who had come to England from Germany, to work with the London Jews Society, and who is remembered today especially for the orphanages he founded. From the beginning, the church which he and others founded (and which met in a chapel called Bethesda), was noted for its good works as well as its teaching. Even more rapid was the growth of the movement in Plymouth (with a membership of some seven hundred) where, because the members gave themselves no name, they became known as "Plymouth Brethren". It is a title they have never accepted. Some in more recent times have accepted the name "Brethren" without the Plymouth, or "Christian Brethren", but even these titles undermine the original intention to be simply Christians rather than another denomination. Incidentally, the bad publicity which occasionally crops up in the media almost always refers to the intolerant attitude of one section which separated in the 1840s and has ever since shown exclusive tendencies. Most of the Brethren churches today would gladly endorse the far-seeing Christian ideals of Groves and Müller. Of Groves we are told: "his remarkable and unaffected humility rendered him quick to see whatever was good in others, slow to condemn". He longed to see "true believers cast aside their denominational differences and exhibit the essential unity of the churches of God". From his experiences in India, he saw a caste system of European missionaries as well as among the Hindus: "It is truly hateful," he wrote, "that one worm should refuse to eat with, or touch, another worm, lest he become polluted". And George Müller warned against thinking: "We are the Church. Truth is only to be found among us. All others are in error".

Archie Boulton would be fourteen years old when George Müller died in 1898. Probably he never met him, though he would have heard of him and his orphanages, and perhaps seen some of the books he wrote. As a young man, Mr Boulton belonged to one of the many Brethren churches on Merseyside, which met in Camden Hall, off Laird Street, Birkenhead. Then he moved to support another Birkenhead group at Ebenezer Street Gospel Hall, perhaps because he found the views of the friends at Camden Hall too rigid in some ways; for example, they held strictly to the idea that women should keep silent, whereas Mrs Boulton insisted on praying aloud in their prayer meetings, with her husband's full approval.

Mr Boulton had his sights on starting a new church (nowadays it would be called "church planting") in Bebington. So he and a few friends met, first of all, in a hay loft on some land belonging to his father. Then Archie bought the land next to it, so that they could put up a building of their own. We have his own words to describe how it came about:

Originally, it was a vacant plot on which two donkeys, belonging to the owner of the land, grazed. Often, with envious eyes I gazed at the site, thinking what a wonderful place it would be for a church. You can imagine my disappointment when I learned that the ground had been sold for housing development. However, I discovered that a builder I knew had bought it, and after some friendly persuasion, he agreed to sell it to me. But when we came to build, a difficulty arose because of its close proximity to houses. The original owner was rather opposed to a church because of the noise churchbells would cause. Assuring him there would be no bells, he dropped his opposition.

The opening ceremony on the 17th September 1927 was a joyful occasion, supported by more than three hundred people from over thirty Brethren churches in Merseyside and beyond. From the beginning, the new church rejected exclusive labels. The notice board said nothing about "Brethren", not even calling the building a "Gospel Hall", as many others did. But it did adopt the name "Bethesda" (which is Hebrew for "house of mercy").

Chris and Eva Walters first came to Bethesda in the mid 1930s. It was not because they knew all about the Brethren. They didn't. It was simply that they were walking to church one Sunday night — they were Methodists — when it began to rain heavily. As they wondered what to do for shelter, they heard singing coming from Bethesda. They went in and, being warmly welcomed, continued during the following weeks and, as it turned out, for several years, until 1942, the year in which their house and shop were destroyed in the blitz, as described by their son Tom, at that time a young nine-year-old. And where was their little boy Tom on that night when they first went to Bethesda? He was far away, not even in England, and had never even met them; for he was not their little boy and he was not English. He was German and he was Jewish.

Chapter 3

A new family

A top priority for every "Gospel Hall", whether it used that name or not, was the need for every individual to make a response to the "Gospel". Very soon Chris and Eva understood this as they had never understood it before. So what began as the attraction of good singing, a shelter from a rainy night and a warm welcome, soon led to a personal commitment to Christ as Saviour and Lord, and they were both baptised to show they really meant it. And with a new-found respect for the authority of the Bible, they read it daily and studied it often. It is probably true to say that (at least until the days of television) the Brethren as a whole had a knowledge of the Bible that was second to none.

Two significant developments stemmed from these priorities. One was a concern to help people who couldn't help themselves. "Love your neighbour as yourself" is an injunction found in both the Old Testament and the New Testament, with the parable of the Good Samaritan added for good measure in case we didn't know who our neighbour was! Jesus in the synagogue at Nazareth read from the scroll of Isaiah to point out that the "Gospel" includes care for the poor, the prisoner and the oppressed. Of course it is not suggested that the Brethren had a monopoly of human kindness, nor on the other hand can it be denied that sometimes they didn't practise what they

preached, for human nature is human nature even among
Brethren. But Chris and Eva were among those who
sincerely believed in putting what they read into practice.
They prayed for guidance and expected God to answer
their prayers.

The other development from a thorough reading of the
Bible was a special interest in the Jews. The Old Testament
— the Jews don't usually call it that, although the
expression "New Testament" actually comes from the Old
Testament, in the Book of Jeremiah; the Old Testament, as
Christians call it, is all about the Jews: their history, their
literature, their victories, their defeats, their glory and their
shame, and especially their unique place in God's plan.
Some Christian groups show an extraordinary interest, not
only in studying the Bible history of the Jews, but in trying
to find detailed clues as to what the future has in store. In
extreme cases this may even lead to an assumption that
wherever Jews and Palestinians are in dispute, the Jews
must be right because God is on their side!

In the early part of 1939, Chris and Eva had a more
practical concern. They put together the compassion of the
Gospel (and no doubt a special respect for "God's chosen
people") with their knowledge of what was going on in
Nazi Germany. No doubt they also saw an opportunity to
fill a gap in their lives, since they had no children of their
own. Could they possibly rescue a child from Hitler's
clutches? How could such a child be found? Would the
German authorities allow it and would permission be
granted by Britain? If there was one pale glimmer of light
in the dark evil of *Kristallnacht* at the end of 1938, it was
that it shook Chamberlain's government into waking up to
the desperate plight of the Jews and taking definite, though
limited, action to rescue their children. Herbert Levy, in his
book *Voices from the Past*, tells how he himself was one of
these children and travelled to London to find safety with

an uncle. He explains that the British government decided to allow entry to ten thousand children, out of a hundred thousand who applied, including many who had not even thought of themselves as Jewish but had one Jewish grandparent and were therefore classified as Jews according to the Nazi rules. A condition imposed by the British government was that every child brought out must be sponsored by an organisation or individual in Britain, who would guarantee that the child would be cared for and not become a financial liability to the State.

As Chris and Eva made discreet enquiries, contact was made on their behalf with the British Society for the propagation of the Gospel among the Jews. They received a letter from the secretary, addressed to Mrs Walters:

2nd February 1939

Dear Mrs Walters,

I have heard from a quarter or two that you are very anxious to adopt a Jewish boy, who is a refugee, and I am submitting to you photographs of a very needy case of a lad who has spent some time in a Jewish orphanage in Germany.

This Home has been told to close down, and as far as I can see by March 1st this lad will have no shelter whatever. I wonder if the boy appeals to you? I think he is seven years of age, but I am not sure.

If you could let me have a word per return I can proceed with the question of applying to the Home Office for him.

May God richly bless you for this generous thought on your part. We have been very burdened with the whole problem.

Very sincerely yours,
(signed) Arthur G. Parry

No doubt a letter accepting the society's offer was sent by return as requested, though it was nearly three months before a further letter was received, this time addressed to both Mr and Mrs Walters, which must have filled them with thankful anticipation:

25th April 1939

Dear Mr and Mrs Walters,

I am happy to give you the good news that at last the permit for Thomas Baumann has come through, and I have wired to Germany to instruct the friends there to apply for a visa forthwith from the British Passport Control Officer in Berlin.

I cannot tell you how long it will be before the arrangements on that side will be complete; it may be a week, it may be a month. I have no doubt that as soon as the visa and other papers are in order the boy will arrive here. I will let you have as long notice as I can as to the date of his coming.

With every good wish,
Yours sincerely,
(signed) Arthur G. Parry

Still more than six weeks passed (and, in retrospect, the time was running out before it would be too late). Then, suddenly, anticipation turned to excitement with the arrival of a telegram on the 12th June: PROMISE ARRIVING TOMORROW JOURNEYING TO YOU WEDNESDAY. And two days later another telegram: ARRIVING WITH TOMMY BIRKENHEAD ONE PM TODAY.

And so Thomas Baumann became Tom Walters, a stranger in a strange land, a seven-year-old representative of the Diaspora. His foster-parents were Chris and Eva

Walters, both born in 1888, so now turned fifty as they welcomed young Tom into their home. And his guarantor, to satisfy the Home Office? None other than Mr Archie Boulton of Bethesda.

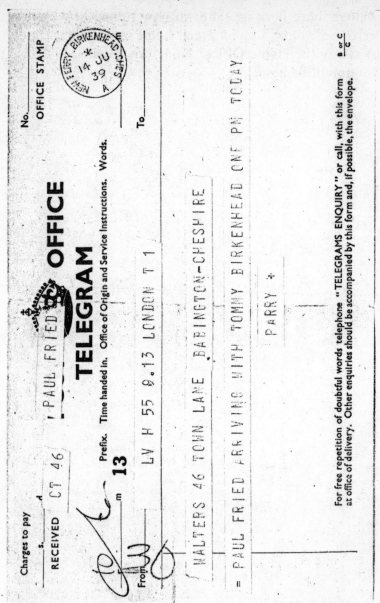

The two telegrams received by Chris and Eva Walters, to announce Tom's imminent arrival, June 1939.

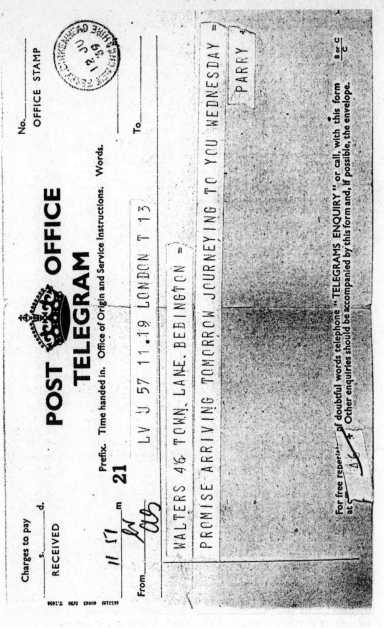

POST OFFICE TELEGRAM

Charges to pay
s. d.
RECEIVED

Prefix. Time handed in. Office of Origin and Service Instructions. Words.

No. OFFICE STAMP

From

To

21

11 57

m
005

LV J 57 11.19 LONDON T 13

WALTERS 46 TOWN. LANE. BEBINGTON =

PROMISE ARRIVING TOMORROW JOURNEYING TO YOU WEDNESDAY =

PARRY +

B or C
C

For free repetition of doubtful words telephone " TELEGRAMS ENQUIRY ", or call, with this form
at office of delivery. Other enquiries should be accompanied by this form and, if possible, the envelope.

Chapter 4

New language, new school, new life

Having overcome the considerable hurdles in the way of getting Tom out of Germany, Chris and Eva were now faced with the practicalities of helping him to settle down in England. The most urgent problem was language: Chris and Eva knew no German and Tom knew no English. Obviously there was no question of sending him to an ordinary school. But Eva was not one to be daunted by the challenge. "She was the dominant influence in my life," says Tom, as she was for many years to come, for him and for others wherever she went. Even in the block of flats in Worthing forty years later where she lived to the age of ninety-six, everybody went with their problems to her. So, in 1939, as soon as Tom arrived, she set to work to teach him English, and with her help he learned quickly. Indeed, so effectively did he learn and such is the subtlety and mystery of human memory that, nearly sixty years later, he speaks no German whatever!

How much did he understand on arrival in England? Did he suffer from an identity crisis? Not at the time, apparently. After all, the affection and stability of his new home gave him a sense of belonging that he had not had before. His mother was dead, so Eva told him; and now she and Chris were his new mother and father and he was to be their son. It was not true that his mother was dead, as Tom was to find out many years later, but Eva and Chris told him in good faith what they thought was true, because they knew that Tom had been in an orphanage.

And how much did Tom know? He knew he was German. He knew he was Jewish and that Jews were in danger in Germany. He knew that Hitler was in charge of Germany and was a wicked man. And he knew, because Eva and Chris told him, that England was at war with Germany. This was another reason for keeping Tom at home at first. They didn't want the outside world to know that they had given help to a German, albeit a child. Only a few friendly customers knew, and of course some of the friends at Bethesda. Other customers must sometimes have wondered why this young boy didn't go to school and seemed to have so little to say for himself. It is possible, of course, that some families might have balanced their resentment against his being German with sympathy for his being Jewish, but Eva and Chris were taking no risks: they kept him in the house; he played on his own. They encouraged him to forget his German background and to think of himself as British. They wanted a completely new life for him. A door had closed; a new door had opened.

Before long special permission was obtained from the Cheshire Education Committee for Tom to be admitted to the Infants School in Bebington, until the summer of 1940, so that he could learn English more quickly. He then attended the Lower Bebington Church School from 1940 to 1941, and from 1942 to 1944 was a pupil of Bromborough Council School. His last full-time education was at the Somerville Preparatory School in Bromborough (a suburb of Birkenhead) from 1945 to 1947, which brought him up to the age of fifteen, the upper age for compulsory schooling at that time. Because he had missed so much formal education, not to mention having to switch from German to English, he was taught in a class where he was much older than the other pupils, most of whom would leave the preparatory school at thirteen, after taking the entrance examination to a "public" school. His report for the Easter term 1946 gives his age as 13 years 10 months, and the average age of the form as 11 years 2 months. To his great credit, his overall position, in a class of fifteen, is 1st. Only 3rd in algebra, and 2nd in Latin, but top of the class in English, history, geography, scripture, arithmetic, geometry and French. Teachers' comments are "very good" throughout; also very good for tidiness, industry and punctuality. However, there is a critical comment under physical training, about the need to use his left foot more and not keep the ball so much in the air. This becomes even worse in the summer term when, despite a keen attitude, batting, fielding and especially catching are all said to be very poor. There is also an exhortation to try and overcome playing with a cross bat. Neither report makes clear what game is being played, so perhaps they didn't tell Tom either!

After their stay in Mr Boulton's sales office in 1942, the family moved several times in and around Bebington, before settling in Hoylake, about ten miles away. Hoylake is on the north-western tip of the Wirral peninsula, on the corner where the Dee estuary meets the Irish Sea, with the Welsh hills opposite. In between Wirral and Wales at this point is Hilbre Island, which can be reached on foot at low tide, but where the incoming tide races in with frightening speed, cutting off sandbanks and unsuspecting visitors who have neglected to check the tide tables. At certain times of the year the gales are furious and the high tides majestic and spectacular. The name Hoylake dates only from about 1850, though the Hoyle-Lake or Hyle-Lake was formerly the name applied to the waters of the Dee estuary, which was once an important anchorage for shipping. In August 1689, the Duke of Schomberg's army sailed in ninety ships from Hoylake to Carrickfergus, and on the 11th June 1690, King William III (William of Orange) embarked from the spot known today as the King's Gap, and followed the same route to Northern Ireland, to defeat James II at the Battle of the Boyne on the 12th July, a date still celebrated by the Protestant Orangemen. By the twentieth century the Dee was no longer suitable for shipping, having long since been superseded by the deeper waters of the Mersey, but in 1939 Hoylake was still important for fishing, with a fleet of over forty boats. At that time the last remains of a submerged forest from a bygone age could still be seen at low water near the slipway where the boats came in, and at that time also, after war broke out, large parts of the shore-line were disfigured with a double row of "dragon's teeth", that is to say, small concrete pyramids, interspersed with barbed wire, to help ward off an enemy invasion. Hoylake was one of the places mentioned by Lord Haw-haw (William Joyce) in his Nazi propaganda broadcasts: "we've not forgotten you, little Hoylake!"

The Walters family lived first of all in a bungalow near one of the railway stations. (With four stations, the Hoylake urban district is still well served by the Mersey Railway.) Then they settled in a larger house right on the promenade, with an outlook over the sands and the sea, calm and peaceful, with bright sunny days and the beauty of sunrise and sunset; or rough and awe-inspiring. And a few hundred yards away, if they wanted it, fresh fish bought straight from the incoming boats.

When Tom left school, he was keen to work and learn a trade, and asked Chris to enquire about a Hoylake firm of bakers and confectioners owned by Mr David Ross, to see if there was a vacancy for him to serve an apprenticeship there. There was, and Tom worked there from 1947 to 1951. It was a family firm. The directors were Mr and Mrs Ross and their two sons, David and Jim. David had served six years in the Royal Army Medical Corps, after being apprenticed in the bakery trade before the war to his father, who many years before had trained as an apprentice to *his* father. Jim had trained as an accountant, after serving four and a half years in the navy; and joined his parents' firm as secretarial accountant in 1948. His father suddenly died that same year, leaving his wife and two sons as directors. Tom continued his apprenticeship under David's leadership. He worked hard, too hard perhaps at times, for a sixteen-year-old. He arrived at 6 am, knocked on the door three times; David opened a window and threw out the key, then Tom started the fires and began to make the dough. He was never late. "Regular and punctual... thorough training in both bakery and confectionery... a good worker" — so runs his leaving testimonial at the end of the four years. He also attended a day-release breadmaking and confectionery course at the Liverpool College of Technology, leading to certification from the City and Guilds of London Institute. Then for his last few months in Hoylake, Tom worked at Simpson's "Busy Bee" bakery and café, receiving as he left the following testimonial: "I have no hesitation in recommending him as an honest, conscientious worker, very willing and a good time-keeper. I am quite sure that whatever his job, he will do his utmost to give satisfaction. I am sorry to lose him and wish him every success in whatever he undertakes to do." At that time neither Mr Simpson nor Tom himself can have had much idea of what he would undertake to do during the next forty years.

One further thing must be said about Tom's status during this period. Until 1948, he was still not legally the son of Chris and Eva Walters. His entry into England was sanctioned by the British immigration authorities "on condition that the holder (of the visa) does not remain in the United Kingdom longer than TWELVE MONTHS". Such a condition became meaningless with the continuation of the war, and even after the war when the appalling fate of the Jews was known. But formal adoption by a British couple would require that the child be naturalised British, and there was no question of naturalisation of a German national during the war. After the war there were thousands who applied, so the legal process of negotiation could take up to three years. On the 1st July 1948, Tom was finally granted naturalisation and adoption by Chris and Eva, taking officially the family name Walters, which he had already used unofficially for nine years.

Eva and Chris Walters, who adopted Tom in
1939 (legal adoption and naturalisation 1948).

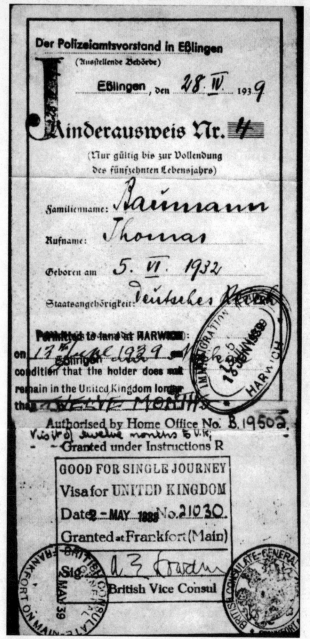

Ticket authorising Thomas Baumann's journey
to the United Kingdom.

Chapter 5

Not by bread alone

Not only did Chris and Eva want Tom to forget his German origins. They also encouraged him to forget that he was a Jew. Looking back on those days, in a programme made by Tyne Tees Television, Tom explains:

> My adopted parents were very kind people. They tried to just take out of me, or away from me, anything to do with the past, anything to do with my Jewish life. Some people may think that they were wrong in what they did and I could probably go along with them a little way, but they were Christians, and they wanted me, more than anything else, to become a Christian.

Christian influence in the home could scarcely have been stronger. Apart from their own contribution, Eva and Chris loved to have people to stay. Tom remembers especially visitors from the Open Air Mission, an organisation of travelling evangelists.

They were not disappointed. It is sometimes said that religion is caught, not taught. For Tom it was both, for Eva believed in both example and explanation. As they sheltered under the stairs during the Birkenhead bombing, they had Bible reading and prayers every night. Eva explained that

she and Chris were not afraid; if they were killed it would
be no problem, they would go to heaven. Tom need not be
afraid either, if he became a Christian by opening the door
of his heart to Jesus and handing his life over to him. "She
put it into the context of a fear", says Tom; "frightened me
into the kingdom". One passage of the Bible was especially
important, a verse from the Book of Revelation:

> 'Behold, I stand at the door and knock. If any man
> hear my voice and open the door, I will come in to
> him and sup with him and he with me.'

Eva illustrated the verse with a picture of Jesus Christ
standing at the heart's door of a person's life, unable to
force his way in, because there is no handle on the outside.
The picture is well-known, painted by Holman Hunt (once
for Keble College, Oxford and, fifty years later, for St
Paul's Cathedral), with the title "The Light of the World".
The risen Christ is holding a lantern in his hand, indicating
that he is able to dispel the darkness from an individual's
life, but only if that person is willing to "open the door".

In later life, Tom came to realise that the original
context of Christ's knocking at the door is not the
conversion of an individual, but a challenge to a lukewarm
church. None-the-less, he is quite happy to say, "Revelation
3:20 brought me to the Lord". His words in the TV
programme reflect his conviction that this was the start of
a lifetime of Christian commitment:

> An amazing thing happened as she read those verses
> because, just then, as it were, God was standing at
> my heart's door and though God couldn't open it, I
> could open it and I just opened my door to Jesus
> Christ, and Jesus came into my life and he's been
> there ever since.

This all happened before the family left Bebington. Then, having escaped the bombs — by a close shave — they found themselves in Hoylake, though Chris travelled to work at Lever Brothers in Port Sunlight (near Bebington), the soap factory and famous model village founded by Viscount Leverhume half a century before.

They quickly settled into the fellowship of the Brethren church, known in the town generally as Wood Street Gospel Hall, later changing its name to Hoylake Chapel. The premises, like those in Bebington, were built by one of the members, in this case as long ago as 1899. The builder was Mr Robert Aldred, who also built houses in several parts of Hoylake, for example in Alderley Road and Stanley Road, named after Lord Stanley of Alderley; also in Cable Road and Valentia Road, named to commemorate the laying of the Atlantic cable from Valentia in western Ireland. Some ten years before building the Hall, Mr Aldred had provided the organ for his young daughter to play, to accompany the singing of the newly-formed church in the days when it met in the Central Hall and used a portable bath for baptisms. When the Walters family arrived, nearly sixty years later, Mr Aldred's daughter was still playing the organ. She was one of many who found it was still possible to "sing the Lord's song" and give faithful service even after personal tragedy, for she would have left the area long before, before the first world war, if her fiancé had not been drowned on the Titanic in 1912.

It was a warm-hearted church with a family atmosphere, though there had been a brief but sad experience some years before, when a group of members left after a dispute over what "holiness" meant in the Christian life, rather like the way that nowadays people argue over the word "charismatic". By the time of the second world war, such disputes were long forgotten. New people had arrived and perhaps the very dangers and stresses of the war helped to draw people together. Some of them were families who, like the Walters, had moved from Liverpool or Birkenhead to escape the bombing. Others already lived in Hoylake, but faced the dangers and destruction of the blitz at their place of work. Mr Andrew Hayley, one of the elders of the fellowship, worked in Liverpool as a tailor, until his property was bombed. Then he was offered premises to rent in West Kirby (part of the Hoylake Urban District). One of the features of the evening Gospel meeting every Sunday was his reading of a long list of names of all the men associated with the fellowship who were serving in the armed forces; followed by a prayer for their protection.

Also from Birkenhead came the Ross family. Their bakery business in Rock Ferry had been bombed as early as the 31st August 1940, on the same night as Wallasey town hall and the Prince of Wales battleship at Cammell Laird's. The family stayed with relatives for a few weeks, then in rented accommodation belonging to Mr Charles Peers, a member of the Brethren church in Heswall who, like Mr Boulton in Bebington, had built many houses as well as the church building. While living in Heswall, Mr Ross worked in a bakery firm in Chester, before buying his own business in Hoylake. He and Mrs Ross had been founder members of the church at Bethesda, Bebington, so they knew Mr and Mrs Walters well. Not only did they willingly accept Tom into the business, but took a personal interest in him. They often took him for a drive into North Wales and went out of their way to encourage him. When Mr Ross suddenly died in 1948, the whole church felt bereaved, for they had lost a gracious friend and Bible teacher.

If Mr Ross was a teacher, his son David was an energetic preacher, who fired Tom's imagination and took him on many a preaching engagement, together with other young men from the church. Sometimes they went as a drama group. One of those in the group remembers that while he himself played the part of an agnostic politician, Tom was the enthusiastic, excitable evangelist trying to convert him. He also recalls how they supported the month-long tent campaign of the popular evangelist Stan Ford in 1949; and, changing the subject, how Tom confided in him that he thought he was falling in love with one of the girls. Another memory seems to support the picture of Tom getting excited. The story goes that when the young people were helping some older members to sort a collection of clothes into parcels for the "Inasmuch" relief work, one of the ladies struck him with her umbrella, and broke it, in an attempt to curb his teasing sense of humour.

Amongst the young people of Tom's age was Larry, who, unlike many others, had not joined the church with his family. It was the football team that attracted him. He had never known his father, whilst his mother, who worked in Birkenhead with the Mersey Railway, had been killed in the blitz when Larry was nine years old. Perhaps he felt some affinity with Tom. He knew that Tom was adopted and that he was Jewish. Significantly, he did not know that he was German. He remembers going round a housing estate with Tom, giving out Gospel tracts and talking to groups of children. He remembers being with at a meeting in Hebron Hall, Wallasey, when Tom explained to the congregation that he had three birthdays: his natural birth, his new life when he came to Britain, and his "new birth" when he became a Christian. Larry also remembers a conversation about money: Tom had firm ideas, even as a teenager, about "tithing", seriously setting aside money from your income for God's work. One of the reasons (thinks Larry) why God has blessed him as he has.

The Hoylake church was active in many ways, and not least the Walters family. There were services for children in two convalescent homes. One of these was led by Mr and

Mrs Richards, who lived in the same road as the Walters, leading down to the promenade. It had been started by Mr and Mrs Hattrick; and Mrs Hattrick, now widowed and very old and very deaf, still enthusiastically went along. She lived right at the end of the promenade, in a house built by her late husband (yet another Brethren builder). She had a stentorian voice, developed in earlier days in the Salvation Army in Birkenhead, and she still led a women's Bible class on Sunday afternoons in Hoylake Chapel, upstairs, while Mr Richards (Tom's Bible Class leader) talked to the young people downstairs.

The service in the other convalescent home was started by Jim Ross and continued under the leadership of Mrs Walters, who also worked with Jim's wife Edna to run a P.E. class for girls, and to give an epilogue at the end of each session. One district of Hoylake is called Meols (from an Old Scandinavian word meaning "the sandhills"), listed in William the Conqueror's Domesday Book. Along a country lane on the outskirts of Meols there was a squatters' camp in the 1940s. Here too Jim and Edna ran a Sunday School and Mrs Walters led a women's meeting during the week.

During the summer months there was open air preaching on the beach every Sunday afternoon, at first to adults from a mobile pulpit. Then in 1949 came Stan Ford. Stan had been the heavyweight boxing champion of the Southern Counties when, shortly before the war, he had had a dramatic conversion after a heart-to-heart talk with a tent evangelist whose meeting he and his friends had planned to disrupt. Now, in his early thirties, 6'2" tall and weighing about seventeen stone, with yellow-blond hair and blue eyes, he was an arresting figure. He was also a compelling preacher, with a naturally loud voice, fluent, witty and challenging. He drew crowds wherever he went. With his experience of the boxing booth of a travelling fair-ground, he was at home in a large tent and had his own marquee for conducting evangelistic meetings. In August 1949 he brought it to Hoylake, where, incidentally, he and his young family had recently come to live. For the whole month he preached in the tent in the evenings and held children's services on the beach in the afternoons, very often with games organised in the morning. His gift for telling Bible stories was especially successful with the children, enlivened with flannelgraph illustrations. He was scornful of microphones and like a caged lion in a conventional pulpit, preferring a more spacious platform indoors and a simple canvas screen on the beach. Following his example, at least in the open air, others adopted the same style for the beach services in the years that followed, catering specially for children, who sat on the sand to listen, while the adults up on the "balcony", that is, leaning on the railings of the promenade, enjoyed it too. Special speakers, including Stan Ford, were invited to take a fortnight of meetings in the school summer holidays, but for the Sunday afternoons throughout the summer, it was David Ross who was the leader, supported by a team of helpers, including Tom.

Chapter 6

Military service and macaroons

There was one more major activity of the church during this time, related directly to the war and, for some years after the war, to military service. In nearby West Kirby there was a large camp of the Royal Air Force, with about four thousand young men in training. They were often at a loose end during the weekend, wandering the streets of Hoylake and West Kirby, looking for something to do, especially on Sundays when the shops were closed. In any case, most of them hadn't much money to spare. The church's initiative was to provide a simple afternoon tea, free of charge, to any who cared to come. Sometimes the invitation spread from one serviceman to another by word of mouth, but there was also far more active publicity. The young men of the church, who were not much younger themselves than the young airforcemen, would go out along the main street to invite them in. Tom Walters was one of the most enthusiastic. He didn't waste words, or beat about the bush, even in those days. "Wanna free tea?" he would say cheerfully, pausing only to make sure they knew where it was. Many a Sunday there would be thirty or forty or fifty who came along, occasionally over a hundred, which caused hectic activity behind the scenes to find extra loaves to slice and butter for the hungry hordes. At the end of the tea a short talk was given. Most of the boys did not stay on after that for the evening service, but nearly all accepted a New Testament which was given free on the understanding that they promised to read it.

For Tom, these air force teas led to a long-standing friendship. One of the visitors, a young man named Alan Jones, evidently did stay for the evening service, and soon got to know the Walters family, and to enjoy their hospitality, when they invited him to their home for a meal. When the time came for his passing-out parade at the end of eight weeks' training, he asked for advice regarding a suitable hotel where his father and mother could stay; and, not surprisingly, Tom's parents replied that they would be delighted to have Alan's parents stay with them. And so they did. Not only so, but soon afterwards, Tom received an invitation to visit them at their home in Tunbridge Wells. Tom wondered at first if this was merely a polite formality, but after two or three invitations, he decided they really meant it and went to stay for a few days. He was astonished to find that their house was a palatial mansion in a private park. Mr Jones was a wealthy man, the owner of a chain of a dozen fishmongers' shops. He took Tom out and showed him the area. Tom came home full of enthusiasm and with an invitation for his parents to go and stay. Chris and Eva were now in their sixties, but they were still prepared to consider setting up their own business, or rather to help Tom to do so and support him in it. The upshot was that they found some premises for sale in the little Kent village of Penshurst, some five miles from Tunbridge Wells, where the three of them set up a bakery and confectionery business.

Alan Jones and his parents were members of the Brethren church in Tunbridge Wells and the Walters family quickly found a spiritual home there. But Mr and Mrs Jones were not the kind to take their Christian faith along to worship on Sundays and then leave it behind when they came home. They believed that if God had given them a beautiful house to live in, it was so that they could use it for God's kingdom. Their hospitality was prodigious. There would often be two dozen people sitting round the large table for Sunday lunch, invited home after the Sunday morning worship. Mr Jones was a good host, cheerful and relaxed: after lunch, with a house full of people, he would slip into one of the unoccupied rooms and lie down on a settee for his afternoon siesta. Then on Sunday evening it was activity again: in one of the spacious rooms a Christian meeting, with a good speaker, for nurses from a nurses' home, with transport laid on to bring them and take them home again.

Tom was actively involved in these gatherings and found a home from home with the Joneses, going every Saturday night and staying till late Sunday night, even though Monday morning would see him up at three or four o'clock to start the breadmaking at Penshurst. He was also following a course at the Bakery Students Society of Croydon Polytechnic and was awarded a diploma in the annual competitions of 1952. The following year he gained a Certificate of Merit in the national Hovis breadmaking competition and a first class City and Guilds qualification for breadmaking. In its own right the Penshurst bakery became well known for the excellence of its sponge cakes and macaroons, Tom's specialities. No secret recipes, he modestly explains, just good old-fashioned ovens. One customer came specially in her chauffeur-driven limousine to buy macaroons; she lived six or seven miles away at Chartwell: Lady Churchill, the wife of the prime minister.

Tom was busy and happy, hardworking and successful. But there was a cloud on the horizon. Since he had been naturalised British, he was now liable for national service, compulsory for all young men (without special reason for

exemption) after their eighteenth birthday. In 1953 Tom
was twenty-one. He had already had his call-up deferred to
finish his professional training, and in April of that year
continued deferment for three months was granted. A
further request in August, however, was refused, and Tom
soon found himself in the army, in the Royal Army
Ordnance Corps. After the usual "square bashing" at
Aldershot, he was sent to Libya, to the British base at
Benghazi, and then to Derna, near Tobruk. At that time
Libya was a "united kingdom", recognised by the United
Nations at the end of 1951, with the former ruler of
Cyrenaica as King Idris I. The country had been an Italian
colony, but passed under British and French
administrations after the defeat of Italy during World War
II. By a twenty-year treaty on the 29th July 1953, shortly
before Tom's call-up, Britain agreed to pay an annual
development grant of one million pounds, and to maintain
military bases. The United States signed a similar treaty the
following year. So Tom was there to help the maintaining!

From his point of view, it was not at all clear what his
contribution was. There was, however, one occasion when
he was called upon to make an unexpected contribution.
Each Sunday there was the "padre's hour" and one week
the padre didn't turn up. The commanding officer, a major,
knew that Tom was a Christian and asked him to take the
service and speak to the men. Tom willingly did so. His
text? Revelation 3:20 — *"I stand at the door and knock.
If any man... open the door, I will come in."*

But on the whole, very little seemed to be expected of the
men, except to be there. There was little or no work to do.
For someone of Tom's temperament, with years of
purposeful activity behind him, the time dragged. And then
news came from home that made his situation worse. The
man who had been taken on to manage the bakery in Tom's
absence had proved unsatisfactory and had to be dismissed.

A second man had been appointed, with the same result. The future of the business was in jeopardy. What was Tom to do? He had no confidence that his superior officers would give him anything other than sympathy, perhaps not even that. What he did do was an early example of his characteristic directness, what would nowadays be called an entrepreneurial spirit: he wrote to the Prime Minister! He told him the urgent need for his presence at the Penshurst bakery (no, he didn't mention macaroons!) and the apparent pointlessness of his sojourn in Libya. His letter evidently struck a chord with Mr Churchill, who had had long experience of flouting rules "when the curmudgeons of red tape interposed their veto" (his own words). Perhaps he remembered the many occasions when his mother had come to his aid to further his career ("in my interest she left no wire unpulled, no stone unturned, no cutlet uncooked"), or when he himself had obtained a commission for his brother in the South African Light Horse; and it must be said that in Churchill's young days it was always a question of pulling strings to get *into* a regiment, rather than get *out* of it. At all events, Tom's request was granted and within six weeks he was back home with a compassionate discharge. Tom's only regret was that his immediate superiors in Libya may have been called to account for negligence, endangering the discipline of the army's hierarchy by allowing his letter to get through. In their defence, their "negligence" may simply reflect a policy of not censoring every private letter, since the letter to Churchill would be enclosed in an envelope addressed to Tom's parents in England, for them to send on.

With his brief military service behind him, Tom set to work once more with characteristic energy. Chris and Eva were now both sixty-five. The business was Tom's responsibility.

The bakery at Penshurst.

Chapter 7

Roots and branches

In 1955 Tom met Judy. She was a children's nurse who came to the Sunday night meetings at the Joneses' house. Tom saw Judy "quietly sitting there", found out that she worked at Dr Barnardo's Home in Tunbridge Wells, and on Tuesday telephoned and asked for Judy. Floored for a moment when asked "Which Judy?", he recovered in time to say, "The one at the nurses' meeting". So they found the right one and she agreed to meet him.

Judy, like Tom, was a committed Christian. She had always gone to church. It was the tradition she was brought up to, not at home but at school. She was the middle one of three sisters, with no brothers, to the disappointment of her father, who had little time for girls and would have liked a son to carry on the family name in business, as he had from his father. He sent the two younger girls to a high class boarding school in Kent. Every Sunday they wore hats and gloves for church parade and walked to the church in a "crocodile". But she had no definite Christian faith of her own until one day, during her college course, she was invited to join a coach party to hear Billy Graham during his 1954 Harringay crusade. She responded to the appeal to go forward and accept Christ as Saviour and Lord, and a new motivation guided her life from that day forward. She joined an evangelical church in

Tunbridge Wells and was confirmed. And of course she was glad to go along to the Sunday meetings at Alan Jones's house. By the end of 1955 Tom had asked her to marry him and she had said yes. Then the next big hurdle was how to raise the question with her father and stepmother (her own mother had died four years earlier).

Henry Waite, Judy's father, was the owner of the firm Waite and Sons, in Mitcham, Surrey, the biggest lampshade manufacturing company in Britain, and possibly in Europe. His factory employed several hundred people and was sufficiently important to be requisitioned by the government during the war to make munitions. Later a second factory was opened in Wales. Customers included the best known stores, such as Woolworth's. So it was not without some trepidation that Tom, in those days penniless by comparison, contemplated the prospect of saying to Henry, "May I marry your daughter?" Tom has a vivid memory of the scene when he did so. It was in a disused railway carriage — sounds like the setting for a famous international peace treaty! but no, it was converted into a holiday home on the Sussex coast where Henry and Nell (Judy's stepmother) were on holiday and had agreed to have a meal with Judy and Tom. The first response was as Tom expected: "What are your prospects?" asked Henry, and if not entirely convinced by Tom's replies, was evidently prepared to give him the benefit of the doubt; recognising at the same time that the young couple's love for one another was of some significance. He gave his consent and Tom and Judy were married on the 22nd April 1957 at Kingswood Church on the private estate at Kingswood, Surrey, where Henry lived. Alan Jones was best man and Tom was particularly pleased that the guests included his own mother's sister, Johanna (or Hanna) Baumann.

Together with his consent, Henry also gave Tom some advice: "If ever you set up in business on your own, choose a good bank manager, a good accountant and a good solicitor". He also put Tom in touch with experienced professionals that he knew and trusted. Up till then, Tom had been managing the Penshurst bakery business that belonged to Chris and Eva. When he married, the business was sold. Chris and Eva bought a house in Jarvis Brook, near Crowborough, which they split into two, upstairs-downstairs (with no social connotation!), to make one flat for themselves and another for the newly-weds. There was a Brethren church nearby where they found Christian fellowship, and Tom went to work for a Mr Futcher, who owned five bakery shops. Before long Tom was "talent-spotted" by Peter Wilkes, the director and senior sales manager of Cranfield Brothers Flour Millers, Ipswich, who made frequent visits delivering flour. "If ever you want to go on your own", he told Tom, "I'll put the money up". He was as good as his word. Tom took up his offer in 1960, explaining it to Chris and Eva, who agreed to retire. The accountants he chose, however, were not his father-in-law's choice, but a firm recommended by the flour millers who had lent him the money. They sent a young , seventeen-year-old articled clerk, Brian Muir, to check up and advise. When later he qualified, he founded a partnership with the firm and became a life-long friend and adviser to Tom. Nearly forty years later, Tom had the painful privilege of being asked to speak at his funeral.

Chris and Eva sold their house and moved to Croyde Bay, near Barnstaple, North Devon. Tom and Judy went to live at Morden, south Wimbledon, and bought a wholesale bakery business at Blackfriars for £2,250. Cranfield Brothers put up the money for the business and the deposit on a house. The main business of the bakery was to make crusty rolls for the newspaper people in Fleet Street. This was ninety per cent of their business; the rest was general confectionery and a shop. They employed two bakers, two vanmen and a lady serving in the shop. Unfortunately, the success of the enterprise was marred by the combined dishonesty of the staff, "cooking the books" and lining their own pockets, so Tom asked Cranfield Brothers to sell the business and find another where Tom would do the bakery and Judy run the shop. This led to a move to Southfields, a bakery making bread only, where the proprietor remained the owner of the premises for a year and taught Tom the business. In characteristic style, Tom was starting work at 3 a.m. each day. Then the freehold came up for sale and was bought by Chris and Eva. Henry stepped in with advice once more and persuaded them to sell it to Tom and Judy, who took his advice and accepted the offer, with the help of an insurance policy whose profits went to Chris and Eva. It proved to be a good investment, still bringing in valuable income as a letting agency several decades later, long after other properties had been bought and sold.

Business was expanding, and so was the family. Jane was born in 1958 and Stephen two years later. In 1962 Tom turned the whole premises into a modern bakery and moved with his family to another house nearby. Philip arrived to complete the family in 1962; then in 1966 they bought a large family house in Wimbledon, near the famous tennis courts, backing onto Wimbledon Park. They bought it for £10,000 and it became the family home for nineteen years, until in 1985 they sold it for £150,000, a sum which went a little way towards the major purchase of Elm House in North Yorkshire. (The Wimbledon house was valued at £350,000 in 1997!) During the twelve years from 1962 to 1974 Tom and Judy acquired thirteen shops: seven bakery shops, including three manufacturing bakeries working round the clock seven days a week, employing a total of 130 people in wholesale and retail selling in Wimbledon, Clapham and Streatham; five launderettes, open seven days a week and in some cases 24 hours a day, employing another fifty or sixty people; one sub post office in one of the bakery shops; one ladies' hairdressing salon and one DIY shop.

It hardly needs to be said that Tom has never been afraid of activity or decision-making. In his own words, "I won't stand still. If something comes along, I take it". And again, "I don't bargain; I buy what I want, at the price asked". And what is Judy's part in all this? It is difficult to imagine such a career of enterprise without a true partnership. And Judy confirms this. They have a joint interest in improving facilities. She agrees that Tom loves buying, but thinks he does himself less than justice if he implies a lack of care about prices. "He has an accurate idea of the valuation of things", is the way she puts it. He certainly has the experience.

In the early days of the bakery, the children were mostly Judy's responsibility, because Tom was so busy. But both of them viewed children as a gift from God. "It's important to be careful how we bring them up, because we have to give account of how we have treated any of his gifts." In early days Philip, the youngest, would be in a lay-back chair in the shop while Judy was serving and Stephen playing on the other side of the "stable" two-panel door into the house. Most afternoons Tom would rest, while someone else looked after the shop and Judy took the children to the park (there was no garden at Southfields). One afternoon a week there was a meeting for mums and toddlers at the house of one of the church members.

From the start she supported and complemented Tom's outlook on life and the outworking of his Christian faith. She sees a shared Christian faith as essential for marriage, though she explains that her faith is simpler than Tom's. His faith is strong, but more subtle. They agree in all essentials. There are no great issues to argue about. Judy recognises that Tom is impulsive, not self-conscious. As for his German Jewish background, that has never been important, but her concern for the welfare of the Jews is equal to his. They are in similar agreement about practical things, like helping the poor. Judy makes this clear:

> I think faith has to be expressed in actions and not just words. We believe that we have been blessed, so we should pass it on. I have this philosophy of leaking buckets: some has to leak out so that more can come in — I'm talking about God's provision, God's blessing. We have been so richly blessed that we should use some of what God has given us to be a benefit to others.

Chapter 8

More roots, more branches

It may seem surprising that Tom's Aunt Hanna was a guest at his wedding, in view of Chris and Eva's policy that he should forget his former family. But in fact when Tom arrived in England in June 1939, Hanna had already been resident in England for some years and was evidently keen to keep in touch, even if frequent visits were not encouraged. Tom met her for the first time (as far as he remembers) before the end of that year.

In 1948, when Tom had to go to the German embassy, she went with him, to prove his identity. She also, with the help of a Jewish solicitor, Dr Oppenheim, began claims for compensation in respect of loss of education, but Chris and Eva wanted no such links with German or Jewish legal systems, or indeed with litigation of any kind. The letter Chris wrote at the beginning of 1952, just after they had moved to Penshurst, has a courteous but formal tone:

> My dear Miss Bowman,
> Many thanks for all your interest in Tom. Both Mrs Walters and myself would rather not put in for any compensation for Tom.
> We shall expect to be seeing you when the weather improves.

Hanna was also active in making claims for compensation on her own behalf, both for loss of career advancement and also for loss of property and fortune. In a detailed attestation drawn up for Dr Oppenheim to submit to the relevant German authorities, she explains how in 1933 the situation of the Jews in Bavaria became so intolerable that she was forced to abandon her home and take steps to emigrate to England. There she found employment as housekeeper and manageress of the Jewish Home for destitute Jewish children in Highbury Grove, London. In September 1935 she went to live in Israel (or Palestine as it was then called), to take charge of the household of her brother Ernst, who lived in Palestine and whose wife had died. But she was destined to live in London, for early in 1937, she went to keep house for Mr Robert Neuberger, a very wealthy member of the Jewish community in Golders Green, who owned copper mines in Australia. His wife had recently died and he had made enquiries among fellow members of the community, to find a person of suitable social background and impeccable references, to look after him and his young daughter Susan. Hanna stayed with him for the rest of his life, more than thirty years. In February 1937 her salary was £100 per annum, not quite £2 per week; by the time she was making her claim for compensation, in May 1955, this had risen to £200 per annum. She was, of course, given free board and lodging in addition (as well as considerable freedom to spend his money as she thought fit), but in her letter supporting her claim, she is at pains to point out: "neither this employment nor the salary corresponds in any way to my former position and professional training".

It is not clear whether she knew at this time that Mr Neuberger had made provision in his will for the rest of her life, but such indeed was the case, as became clear when he died in the early 1970s. The rest of his estate went to his daughter Susan, now living in America. Whilst in his employment Hanna was also active in voluntary work: for five years secretary of "School Care Committees" of the Queensbury Road Secondary Mixed School; and for a while a once-a-week duty in charge of the "Invalid Children's Aid Association". She also gained a diploma in social studies from the University of London. And as early as 1938 she had been a voluntary worker for the "Co-ordinating Committee for Refugees" in London, whose members included organisations run by Jews, Catholics, the Society of Friends (Quakers) and others specially concerned at that time to help refugees from Germany, Austria and Czechoslovakia.

It is good to know that after their marriage Tom and Judy determined to establish a closer friendship with Hanna, so for the next twenty years they met about four times a year, either at their house or her house or at an arranged venue. Tom also took up her offer to help claim compensation for loss of education and received from the Claims Office (*Entschädigungsamt*) in Berlin the sum of DM 5,000 (£427), less £42.14s.0d solicitor's fees, at the beginning of 1960. A similar sum (DM 6,450) was granted as "compensation"(!) for his own mother's loss of freedom. Tom now learned from the compensation office in Berlin that his mother's last address was Number 4, Große Hamburger Straße, Berlin; that she was deported "to the east" (*Ost-Transport*) on the 9th December 1942, to "an unknown destination" (*Ziel unbekannt*) and that she was known to be deceased on the 8th May 1945 — the day after the war in Europe ended. How he would have loved to know more, yet at the same time preferred not to know, for he had long since heard of Auschwitz, and neither he nor Hanna had much doubt about Eva's real destination.

In February 1977 Tom received a phone call from Mrs Susan Koenigsberg, Robert Neuberger's daughter: "Hanna has died. The funeral is today". Tom was her next of kin, but Susan as her foster-daughter was contacted in the USA and had come over to London. Tom hurried off to the funeral. His last links with his mother had gone; but by meeting Susan a new door of friendship and information was opened. She also put him in touch with a cousin of his mother's, Dr Heinz Brühl of San Diego, California. Heinz's mother and Eva's mother were sisters. He, like Hanna, had left Berlin in 1933, but in his case it was to practise as a physician and paediatrician in Hupeh, central China, until in 1948 he took his family to the USA; they became American citizens and he took charge of a large State institution for mentally retarded children. And now from the other side of the Atlantic Tom was to learn more about the family he had lost.

Chapter 9

Brave new world

Tom's great-grandfather emigrated from Posen to the United States in 1852. Posen was the German name for Poznan, a town in western Poland, but ruled by the Prussians after their victory at Waterloo in 1815. There had been a policy of settling Germans in Poland ever since the days of Frederick the Great. German rule became increasingly harsh after several attempts at revolt and by the early twentieth century Polish children were beaten at school for refusing to say the Lord's prayer in German (speaking Polish was banned). Perhaps it was the tension that followed the uprising of 1848 that made great-grandfather want to seek another homeland. His name was Philip Beer. He crossed the Atlantic in a sailing vessel, and eventually found his way over the Rockies to California, taking part in the goldrush as he went. When he arrived in America, he changed his name to Bowman. It is not clear whether he had always been dissatisfied with his name, or simply that he deemed it inappropriate for his new surroundings; anyway Bowman was the name of an uncle already living in the States, so he decided to adopt it.

There is something strangely uprooting about changing one's name. And because it uproots, it may also represent a planting, a branching out into something new. Names have always been important for the Jews: they look to

Abraham, Sarah, Isaac, Jacob, Moses, David, and above all to Israel, the new name given to Jacob, father of the Israelites. Names of places too: Bethel (the "house of God" where Jacob's name was changed), Ebenezer, Hebron, and above all Zion, the psalmists' and prophets' poetic name for Jerusalem, idealised city of David and symbol of God's everlasting protection of his chosen people. The importance of a name is reflected in the ten commandments: "Thou shalt not take the name of the LORD thy God in vain". The Jews of old took this so seriously that for centuries they avoided saying God's name altogether, lest they unwittingly take it in vain; so that they even forgot how to pronounce it, substituting the word "Adonai" in the synagogue Scripture readings, a practice which continues to this day.

This century has seen many changes of names by famous people, for a variety of reasons: Lenin, Stalin, Tito (to create the image of a strong leader); Cliff Richard, Cilla Black, Ringo Starr (to help pop-star publicity); Muhammed Ali, the boxer (as a repudiation of his slave name and a declaration of human dignity and religious conversion); and in 1914 Guelph changed to Windsor and Battenberg to Mountbatten, to avoid the perceived scandal of a nation at war with Germany, led by a royal family with German names. These pressures were still in the future when Philip Beer arrived in America, but the need to integrate into his new environment was a powerful motive. He became Philip Bowman and, after his adventures in California, married and settled down to become an American citizen in South Carolina, where his first children were born: Anna Kaempfer in 1860 and Benno in 1861. By then he was the owner of a cotton plantation, whose workers would be negro slaves. Anna Kaempfer, who many years later returned to America and whose children and grandchildren were all American citizens by birth, always told that she had a negro slave as a wet nurse.

Life in the New World seemed full of promise. The family moved to Richmond, Virginia, where Philip became chairman of the freemasons' lodge. But the political situation was far from promising. The young nation was being torn apart by tension and at the heart of the tension was the slavery question. The southern States allowed slavery; the northern States did not. Many people in the north actively encouraged slaves to escape and make their way to Canada, as graphically presented in Harriet Beecher Stowe's anti-slavery novel *Uncle Tom's Cabin*, which had a tremendous impact when it was first published in 1852, the very year in which Philip Bowman had come to America. By 1860 the population of the northern States was nineteen million, and the southern States twelve and a half million, including four million negroes. The year before, John Brown (later immortalised in the song "John Brown's body") had been hanged for attacking the arsenal at Harper's Ferry to get arms for a slave revolt. Abraham Lincoln tried to find a compromise between the North and the South, but when he was elected president, seven States withdrew from the Union, led by South Carolina. They wrote a new constitution for the "Confederate States of America", one of whose tenets was to prohibit legislation against slavery. The new leaders attacked and destroyed Fort Sumter at Charleston Harbour, causing Lincoln to call for 75,000 volunteers to suppress the revolt. The American Civil War had begun. Other States, including Virginia, joined the Confederacy, which had its capital at Richmond.

Philip Bowman joined the Confederate army, fighting under the leadership of General Robert Lee, who had considerable success at first, but was eventually forced to retreat, first at Antietam, then notably at Gettysburg,

Pennsylvania. Lincoln had already proclaimed the emancipation of all slaves; now he delivered his famous Gettysburg address, with its resolve "that these dead shall not have died in vain — that this nation under God shall have a new birth of freedom — and that government of the people by the people for the people shall not perish from the earth". There had been terrible losses on both sides, about 600,000 dead in all. In addition the towns of the South had been devastated by General Sherman's deliberate policy of destruction. Richmond was one of the towns that lay in ruins. Philip Bowman must have wondered what new birth of freedom had been achieved. On the 9th April 1865 General Lee surrendered and the war was over. Five days later President Lincoln was assassinated. The Bowman family moved to Philadelphia in Pennsylvania, where a third child, Louis, was born on October 31st. Philip Bowman had lost most of his money. His American dream had turned sour. The commander-in-chief of the civil war Union Army, Ulysses Grant, was elected president. Philip decided to take his family back to Germany, when Louis was about six years old. At first they had a farm in Filehna, in the Netze district about forty-five miles north-west of Posen, but by the turn of the century Louis was living in Berlin. He had married Clara Treumann and they had three children, all born in Berlin: Ernst Philip in 1900, Johanna Mathilde (known as Hanna) in 1901 and Eva Felicitas in 1904. Grandfather Philip lived until 1917. Heinz Brühl, Clara's nephew, remembered him as "a man in his eighties, portly, vigorous, a very impressive personality".

Like his father, Louis had a flair for business and, unlike his father, did not find himself embroiled in a disastrous civil war. But there were tensions in Germany too: writing many years later from London, his daughter Hanna says, "I had to change my name to Baumann at the beginning of the war in 1914, as my name Bowman sounded too English!" Her brother Ernst and her sister Eva evidently did the same. They would all be still at school, where names can be a sensitive issue. But their father did not change, except his first name, from Louis to its German equivalent Ludwig. He had become an extremely successful businessman as a broker at the Berlin corn exchange, trading under the name of Ludwig Bowman. He also owned a large estate in Lechbruck bei Füssen, in Bavaria. By 1927, at the age of sixty-one, he had made his fortune and decided to retire to Bavaria. But not before he had drawn up careful legal documents to protect his own interests, as well as those of his family. He invited his son Ernst into partnership in the firm. The legal document, like all legal documents, sounds very formal, the more so because of the difference in the surnames: "Mr Ernst Baumann will become (from 1st April 1927) a partner of Mr Ludwig Bowman in the business" and, significantly, "Mr Ernst Baumann recognises that he, through his admission as co-partner of the fine long-established firm at such a young age and with a comparatively modest investment share, has secured a considerable advantage. For that reason he thereby relinquishes in favour of Mr Ludwig Bowman, his father, his legal right of succession. Mr Ludwig Bowman hereby accepts this renunciation." Other clauses stipulate that certain securities constituting Ludwig's private wealth were not to be disposed of or traded by Ernst without his father's consent. So Ludwig protected his own fortune and Ernst inherited the business but not the rest of his father's wealth. The farm in Bavaria was to be left to his two daughters, who now shared with him the comfort and luxury and status of living at the Gut Kurzenhof, surrounded by the beautiful mountains and lakes of Bavaria, on the Austrian border. Hanna records (6th January 1955):

My father's fortune was so large that he explained to us children that we need not worry about our future, that we could live comfortably off our interest rates.

Another brave new world had begun.

Johanna Bowman (Aunt Hanna).

Eva Bowman aged eleven
(February 1916).

Ludwig Bowman (Eva's father), May 1931, the
month before he died.

Chapter 10

The songs of Zion

John Newton, the former slave-trader who wrote the words of the top-of-the-pops hymn, "Amazing Grace", was the author of many hymns, including the following, based on Psalm 87:

> Glorious things of thee are spoken,
> Zion, city of our God...
>
> Saviour, if of Zion's city
> I through grace a member am;
> Let the world deride or pity,
> I will glory in Thy Name.

Here is a Christian taking over the Jews' reverence for names, and particularly the divine Name. Newton died in 1807, during the Napoleonic wars. He would have been astonished to know that just over a hundred years later churches in Britain, and particularly in Merseyside, were threatened with having their windows broken if they didn't stop singing that hymn. The reason? Not its reference to Zion, though for some that would be provocation enough because of their fear of Zionist extremists. No, it was the tune that caused offence. That hymn was sung, and still is, to the tune "Austria", written by the famous Austrian composer, Franz Joseph Haydn, and known in today's world as the German national anthem, *Deutschland über alles*. The tune was banned in Britain during the first world war by popular opinion. At the same time as Ludwig Bowman's Berlin neighbours were protesting about their fellow-citizens having English-sounding names, there was a furious wave of anti-German feeling in Britain. In Liverpool there were riots in the streets, smashing the windows of German shopkeepers. Mr Weisse, the headmaster of the Liverpool Institute, changed his name to Whitehouse.

How difficult it is to draw a line between patriotism, nationalism and racism! The original sense of *Deutschland über alles* was doubtless an expression of loyalty and service, an emotional, affectionate attachment to the land of one's birth, in the same spirit as Cecil Spring Rice's hymn,

I vow to thee, my country,
All earthly things above,
Entire and whole and perfect,
The service of my love.

It was written as long ago as 1841, by Hoffmann von Fallersleben, on the then British Island of Helgoland and entitled by him simply *Lied der Deutschen* (song of the German people) and not officially adopted as the German national anthem until 1922. It is interesting to speculate what Victoria and Albert thought of it, with their loyalty to both countries. By the outbreak of World War I, it was seen in Britain as an expression of German aggression. After Germany's humiliation, the words played into Hitler's hands, with his arrogant doctrine of an Aryan super-race led by Germany, supported by a policy of conquest and, eventually, extermination. Modern

Germany has sought to erase this impression by adopting, in 1950, only the third verse of the hymn, with its unimpeachable words:

Einigkeit und Recht und Freiheit
für das deutsche Vaterland,
danach lasst uns alle streben,
brüderlich mit Herz und Hand.
Einigkeit und Recht und Freiheit
sind des Glückes Unterpfand.
Blüh' in Glanze dieses Glückes,
blühe deutsches Vaterland.

(Unity and justice and freedom
for the German Fatherland
let us all strive for,
fraternally with heart and hand.
Unity and justice and freedom
as the pledge of happiness stand.
Flourish in splendour this happiness,
flourish German Fatherland.)

It is hard to imagine Adolf Hitler having much enthusiasm for these benign words, or if he had, it would be only after excluding from their scope the minority groups which he hated and despised, in particular the Jews. For Hitler, patriotism meant national fanaticism, in which racial prejudice played a key rôle — a prejudice exhibited for all the world to see at the 1936 Olympic Games in Berlin, when he refused to shake the hand of Jesse Owens, the black American athlete.

Just as in South Africa and in the "slave" states of America, it was often difficult to tell who was black and who was white, so it is not always easy to say who is a Jew and who is not. Officially, in orthodox Jewry,

anyone whose mother is a Jew is Jewish. Nazi Germany
had a wider definition, classifying as a Jew anyone who
had at least one Jewish grandparent. It has often been
pointed out how remarkable it is that the Jews are still a
clearly identifiable people after almost two millennia of
being integrated as citizens of most of the countries of
the world, without a home country of their own. In spite
of this, a definition of Jewishness is not easy. Some Jews
(or modern Israelis) live as materialistic atheists, just
like their Gentile contemporaries, yet have a strong
sense of belonging to their ancient heritage. Others, like
Tom Walters, have become Christians. Does their
acceptance of Jesus as the Messiah make them more
Jewish or less? Some of their orthodox fellow-Jews
would write them off as renegades, but perhaps even
they would agree with the apostle Paul's words: "a man
is not a Jew if he is only one outwardly... No, a man is
a Jew if he is one inwardly, and circumcision is
circumcision of the heart".

At the end of the nineteenth century, the Treumanns
were a well-established Jewish family living at Waren, on
Lake Müritz, some sixty miles north-west of Berlin.
Moritz Treumann and his wife Mathilde (née Moritz) had
three daughters: Trude (Gertrud), Anna and Clara. All
three went to live and have families of their own in Berlin.
Trude married Alfred Brühl, Anna married Gustav Brühl
and Clara married Ludwig Bowman. In a letter written
many years later, Heinz Brühl, son of Anna and Gustav,
paints a picture of a happy extended family, as he and his
brother Hans were "playmates and childhood
companions" of their cousins Ernst, Hanna and Eva, the
children of Clara and Ludwig, both in Berlin and at their
grandparents' home in Waren.

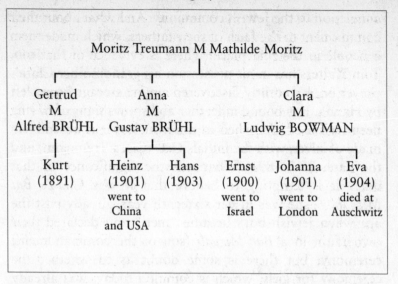

The families were not only happy, but talented and prosperous. Heinz Brühl's cousin Hanna (Johanna), Tom Walters' aunt, writes: "Our mother came from a very wealthy family; her father was a businessman in Waren on the Müritz, Mecklenburg-Schwerin; an uncle of ours was Professor Brühl, a well-known ear, nose and throat specialist; and another uncle was the owner of the very well-known Brühl lace and handcrafts shop in Berlin". Heinz Brühl himself trained as a paediatrician, went to China in 1933 where he was in private practice until 1948 (significant dates politically in Germany and then in China), then went to the United States, where he became director of a large State institution for mentally retarded children.

Such families as the Brühls, the Treumanns and the Bowmans typify the status and influence of Jews in pre-Hitler Germany (as in other European countries). They were loyal citizens of the German fatherland; they were also strongly committed with deep affection and conviction to the Jewish community. And what about their commitment to the faith of their fathers, which made them a people in the first place? There is evidence of that too. Tom Walters has in his possession his grandmother Clara's prayer book, recently discovered among storage boxes left by Hanna. It is bound in leather and shows signs of having been well used. Attached to the front cover is an emblem made of silver, with the initials C.T. (Clara Treumann) and the date: 29.3.1891. What was the significance of that date? It is tempting to believe that it was Clara's *Bat Mizvah* — she was in her sixteenth year, already past the age when Jewish boys became "men" and declared their own faith, in a *Bar Mizvah* (son of the commandment) ceremony; but there is some doubt as to whether the ceremony for girls, which is common today, was already taking place so long ago. If not, perhaps it was a foretaste of the *Bat Mizvah* (daughter of the commandment), promoted by the family or by the person who gave Clara the book. The book contains psalms and hymns and prayers, with the order of service for special days; for example, *Rosch Haschanah*, the New Year. This service, like many others, includes the central Jewish affirmation of the Unity of God, known as the *Shema'*. One of the hymns is a favourite of generations of Christians, as well as Jews, a paraphrase of the twenty-third psalm:

> *Der Herr ist unser Hirt.*
> (The Lord is our Shepherd)

Inside the front cover of the book, in modern German handwriting (Clara's own?) are some lines from Psalm 92:

> *Schön ist's, dem Herrn zu danken,*
> *und seinem Namen zu lobsingen,*
> *am Morgen seine Huld verkünden,*

am Abend seine Treue; denn
erhaben sind seine Werke, der in
den Höhen thront in Ewigheit.

(How beautiful it is to give thanks to the Lord,
and to sing praises to his name;
in the morning to proclaim his grace,
in the evening his faithfulness;
for his works are sublime,
who in the highest is enthroned for ever.)

Inside the back cover are two passages, written in the old
German script (perhaps by one of Clara's parents, or an
older member of the family?); one of them is a quotation
from "Vth Moses" (that is, Deuteronomy):

Der Ewige, unser Gott, schloß mit uns einen Bund
am Horeb. Nicht bloß mit unsern Vätern schloß der
Ewige diesen Bund, sondern auch mit uns, die wir
heut hier alle versammelt sind.

(The LORD our God made a covenant with us in
Horeb. Not only with our fathers did the LORD make
this covenant, but also with us, who are all gathered
here today.)

And the other passage, also inside the back cover, in that
same old-style writing, is the Jewish creed, with its
repeated, "I believe with perfect faith...

in God the only One...
that God has given Man a free will...
that God has chosen Israel to be the witness of God
among the nations..."

...and with its threefold commitment of reverence, justice and personal integrity; finally with its defiant resolve:

> in my last hour I will shout with joy,
> *Shema' Yisrael, Adonai Elohenu, Adonai Echadh!*
> (Hear O Israel, the LORD our God is one LORD).

Every student of Jewish history knows that in the last desperate hours of Simon Bar-Kochba's revolt against the Romans who were besieging Jerusalem in 135 AD, Rabbi Akiba died with the words of the *Shema'* on his lips. Since that day, when all Jews were expelled from Jerusalem, destined to be without a homeland for eighteen centuries, there have been many periods of persecution of the Jews, who have wandered from country to country in search of religious freedom. One such period occurred in the time of Moses Maimonides, the twelfth-century spiritual leader who composed the creed. Not even he, however, saw anything to compare with the scale of persecution under the Nazi régime. How many during those dark days could find comfort in the songs of Zion? How many were able to cling on to the faith that God had chosen Israel to be his witness among the nations? How many Jews in Hitler's death camps shouted, or whispered, or gasped the *Shema'* with their last breath?

Eva's maternal grandparents, Moritz and Mathilde Treumann,
with their youngest daughter (Eva's mother) in Waren, 1890.

Gottesdienſt

für

den Vorabend des Neujahrsfeſtes.

(Roſch haſchanah.)

Chor.

Wie lieblich, ihr Kinder des Herrn, iſt eure heilige Stätte,
Wie lieblich das Haus, der Andacht geweiht.
Auf, mein Gebet, ſteige zu Gott empor,
Daß Er gnädig mich erhöre;
Allgnädiger! ſei mein Schuh, mein Heil.

Vorbeter.
Lobet und preiſet den allmächtigen Gott!

Chor und Gemeinde.
Lob und Preis ſei Gott, dem Allmächtigen!

Vorb. Geprieſen ſeiſt Du, Ewiger, unſer Gott, Herr
der Welt, auf deſſen Wort die Schleier des Abends
ſinken, durch deſſen Weisheit die Himmelspforten ſich
öffnen, der Du die Stunden dahin fließen, die Zeit
dahin wandeln und die Geſtirne ihren Kreislauf vollenden
läſſeſt am Firmament. Schöpfer des Tages und der
Nacht, der Monde und der Jahre, nach Deinem Willen
rollt Tag und Nacht dahin, und was in ihnen entſteht,
geht wieder unter auf Dein Geheiß. Du aber, Gott,

biſt ewig, unveränderlich immerdar, und walteſt über
uns für und für. Geprieſen ſeiſt Du, Ewiger, der Du
der Zeiten Lauf geordnet.

Chor u. Gemeinde. Amen.

Vorb. Mit unwandelbarer Liebe haſt Du uns geliebt,
und ewige Wahrheiten in Geſeh und Lehre uns offen=
bart; darum, durch alle Zeiten halten wir an Deinem
Worte feſt und freuen uns Deiner Lehre für und für.
Denn ſie iſt das Leben und an ihr hangen wir in
frohen und in trüben Tagen. So wende auch Deine
Liebe nicht ab von uns in Ewigkeit. Geprieſen ſeiſt
Du Ewiger, der Du uns in Liebe Deine Lehre ver=
liehen haſt.

Chor u. Gemeinde. Amen.

(Die Gemeinde erhebt ſich.)

Vorbeter.

שְׁמַע יִשְׂרָאֵל יְהֹוָה אֱלֹהֵינוּ יְהֹוָה אֶחָד׃

Chor und Gemeinde wiederholt.

Vorbeter.

בָּרוּךְ שֵׁם כְּבוֹד מַלְכוּתוֹ לְעוֹלָם וָעֶד׃

Chor und Gemeinde wiederholt.

Vorb. Höre Iſrael: Gott, unſer Gott, iſt der ein=
zige, ewige Gott! Geprieſen werde Sein Name,
Sein Reich und Seine Herrlichkeit in Ewigkeit. Du
6*

From Clara's prayer book: Order of Service for the New Year (*Rosch
Haschanah*). The first line of Hebrew on the right-hand page is the *Shema'*.

> Schön ist's, dem Herrn zu denken,
> und seinem Namen zu lobsingen;
> am Morgen seine Huld verkünden,
> am Abend seine Treue; denn
> erhaben sind seine Werke, der in
> den Höhen thront in Ewigkeit.

Handwriting in the front of Clara's prayer book:
It is good to give thanks to the Lord…

Der Herr ift unfer Hirt,
Und wir find Seine Heerde;
 Zur Weide gab er uns
Die prachterfüllte Erde.
 Und dürstet wo ein Herz,
Er weift es an die Quelle;
 Es findet Labung dort
An Gott geweihter Stelle.

 Durch Todesnacht und Graun
Wir unerschrocken gehen;
 Sein Auge schützet uns,
Läßt uns nicht untergehen;
 Sein Arm verschafft uns Sieg,
Bereitet Freud' und Segen;
 Sein Schutz verläßt uns nie
Auf allen unfern Wegen.

 So folgen Freud' und Luft
Uns nach auf allen Wegen;
 Es wächft, wohin wir schau'n,
Des Himmels reicher Segen.
 Er schmückt das Leben uns
Mit Gaben Seiner Gnade,
 Bis einft wir ewig ruh'n
Nach langem Pilgerpfade.

Paraphrase of the twenty-third psalm,
in Clara's prayer book.

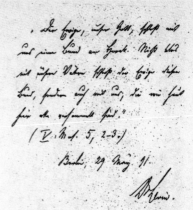

Quotation from Deuteronomy about
the Covenant, written in the back of
Clara's prayer book.

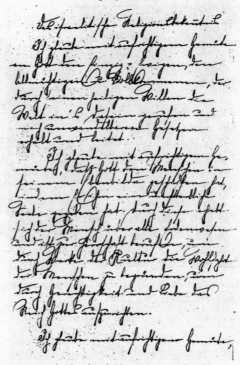

Part of the Jewish creed, written in the back of Clara's prayer book.
Those who are practised in old German handwriting will recognise the
first two words of each paragraph: *Ich glaube* (I believe)...

Clara's prayer book (now in Tom's possession), with inscription
etched in silver: 29.3.1891.

Chapter 11

The lights of Europe go out

Sadly, Clara died in 1917, the same year as her father-in-law, Philip Bowman, although she was only forty-three. Her younger daughter Eva, until then a pupil at Frau Kollmorgan's school in Kleiststrasse, Berlin, now took over the running of her father's household, in Nürnberger Platz; quite a responsibility at the age of sixteen, although, as Hanna recalls, they had two servants. Hanna, three years older than Eva, continued her education and vocational training: "as I had a particular interest in farming and biology, I attended the fruit-growing and horticulture school for well-bred ladies in Berlin-Marienfelde". Lectures on horticulture and cattle breeding followed at the agricultural nightschool in Berlin and also, in 1921, voluntary work on a fruit farm. On the strength of all this training, Hanna was able to take over the management of her father's Kurzenhof estate at Lechbruck in Bavaria. He must have been proud to have two such capable daughters.

Ernst continued to run the business in Berlin, but by the early thirties he had left Germany for Palestine. Like his sister Hanna, he felt and anticipated the sinister atmosphere of discrimination against Jews. When he saw notices in public gardens saying that entrance was forbidden to Jews and dogs, he decided it was time to leave. He had already visited Palestine some years before, and now hoped to start a new life there. But sadness struck before long, as his wife Detta died in 1935, leaving him with a four-year-old son to look after.

Meanwhile, in Germany, Hitler's National Socialist Party was growing ever stronger and more ruthless. In 1938 Czechoslovakia was invaded, on the pretext of an appeal for help from the large German population of Sudetenland. Many Jews hastily fled from the country; among them a young couple from the city of Cheb, on the German border (now in the Czech Republic). With their infant son Daniel, they boarded a ship destined for Palestine, but the British navy, with orders to prevent a flood of immigrants into a politically volatile area (then under British mandate), fired on the ship. Tragically, Daniel's father was killed. His young widow Trude, however, arrived safely with her little boy and before long met and married Ernst Baumann, who gladly adopted Daniel and brought him up with his own son Joel. Nearly sixty years later, in 1997, thanks to the wonders of E-mail and fax machines, news of Daniel has come to light. He is professor of geography and environmental development at the Ben-Gurion University of the Negev. He is of course (by adoption) Tom Walters' cousin and in a faxed reply to Tom's enquiry makes revealing comments about Ernst:

> I understand that he felt very early, what many did not want to, that there was no future for Jews in Germany, in spite of the fact that he was very deeply rooted in German culture. I was in very good relations with him and for many years I did not know that he was my stepfather.

The only member of the family to stay in Germany after Hitler came to power was Eva. Her father Ludwig had died at the beginning of June 1931. Later that same year she had a relationship with a man that had far-reaching consequences, of which the most significant was the birth of a little boy, Thomas, in June 1932. He was destined to live most of his life in England, but more than sixty years later he felt the restlessness of an identity crisis. There were many unanswered questions:

Who was his father? What was his name? Why did he and Eva not get married? Perhaps because he was not Jewish, although it was not until four years later that the Nürnberg laws forbade marriage between Jews and persons of "German blood"; forbade indeed cohabitation, in or out of wedlock, between Jews and "Aryans". And what about Tom's grandfather's attitude — did he know about the relationship before he died? Did he disapprove of it? If so, he did nothing to "disinherit" his daughter. And in any case he died before she became pregnant. There seemed little doubt that sister Hanna disapproved, but was her disapproval chiefly because the man was an Aryan, a Gentile? She writes, twenty-five years later, as though she were not quite sure that he was, saying that her nephew "was at least half Jewish" and that the father "was an Aryan, as far as I know." But anyway, the pregnancy itself was considered a scandal, and Hanna comments:

> My sister could not stay at a little place like Lechbruck and changed her place of residence to Berlin, where she lived with friends at Lützowstrasse.

Perhaps Hanna also felt resentment that she was now left with sole responsibility for managing the estate at Lechbruck, not to mention selling it, at a time when unprecedented pressures and problems had to be faced.

Eva evidently thought that she would be safely anonymous among the 160,000 Jews of Berlin, safe from scandalised friends and neighbours and safe from the limelight of growing racial discrimination. But if for the time being she had found safety in numbers, she was also perilously insecure, and far more than she realised. Could she at this stage have left Germany, as her brother and sister did? It was the year before Hitler took supreme power. She chose to stay. She had her little boy to look after, as well as herself, and needed to find employment.

It may safely be assumed that she took no active interest in politics, but she would be well aware of Hitler and the activities and policies of the National Socialist Party. It was largely in Bavaria, where Eva and her sister lived, that Hitler's dramatic rise to power had taken place. After leaving hospital in 1919 (he had been wounded and gassed during the war), he had joined the German Workers' Party in Munich, which the following year changed its name to the *Nationalsozialistische Deutsche Arbeiterpartei* (whose members became known as "Nazis"). From then on, his skill in oratory and in manipulating people and movements fired his thirst for power and his belief that all men are not equal, nor nations, nor races. For Hitler, democracy was folly, as was the Communist ideal of a classless society. Nationalism, not internationalism, was what mattered. A nation-state of "Aryan race" was all-important, and the greatest of these was Germany led, of course, by himself. The Jews, even more than the Communists, were to be treated as enemies, banished or destroyed. As early as April 1933, new laws dismissed all Jews from the civil service and universities and from entering the professions, and these laws were progressively tightened with supplementary decrees during the next few years. The plan was to force Jews to emigrate, to make Germany "Jew-free". Various countries that might receive them were discussed: Rhodesia, British Guiana, the United States, even a State of Israel in Madagascar! However, the now famous "scrap of paper" meeting with Britain's Neville Chamberlain at Munich in

1938 (and with Daladier from France) convinced Hitler that he could use the Jews to further his own ambitions. Gerald Reitlinger comments in his book, *The Final Solution*:

> They (the Jews) were henceforward not merely prisoners... waiting to be ransomed, but future hostages for any political demands that Hitler might make on other countries. Hitler's unexpected success must have made him revise his views on Jewish emigration. He must have reflected that what he called 'International Jewry' would be less inclined to pull the strings of interventionist war if he kept some hundreds of thousands of Jews in pawn and showed what he might be prepared to do with them.

It seems that Hitler had already planned to carve up Poland, taking a large part into the German Reich and expelling all its Jews (over two million) into the part that was left, as a first step towards "the final solution of the Jewish problem". Those grim words, "the final solution" (*die Endlösung*) were used in a report circulated by Reinhard Heydrich, the chief of the Secret Police, part of the Secret Political Police (Gestapo) founded by Hermann Göring. Heydrich was, so Reitlinger says, "the real engineer of the Final Solution", all the more bitterly ironical if the rumours are true that one of his grandmothers was Jewish and that he had a new headstone put on her grave with the name "Sarah" removed. From January 1939 Heydrich supervised the emigration of Jews from Germany. Did he authorise the departure of seven-year-old Tom Walters in June 1939? And from October 5th 1938, only a week after the Munich agreement with Chamberlain, a law was passed requiring the passports of Jews to be stamped with the letter "J". The sinister aspect of this last law was that it was requested by "neutral"

Switzerland, to prevent a flood of Jewish immigrants, whilst at the same time protecting the tourist industry (for non-Jews) between Germany and Switzerland. The child's identity card issued to Tom Walters on the 28th April 1939 is clearly marked with a "J", although at that date plans were afoot to take him to England, so there was not much danger of his being an unwanted visitor to Switzerland.

To the policy of emigration was soon added expulsion and extermination. The museum of Yad Vashem in Jerusalem gives a stark summary of what happened:

> Hitler decided that the "Final Solution to the Jewish Problem" was to murder every Jew who fell into Nazi hands... Most of those who planned this genocide were seemingly ordinary members of society and, in the main, educated men. They were, however, inculcated with the belief that every Jew was a powerful enemy of the German people and had to be destroyed. As a result, they planned the execution of a crime unparalleled in human history.

After Hitler's invasion of the Soviet Union in 1941, special army units were given the task of eliminating "hostile elements". One group commander admitted murdering 90,000 Jews on the orders of Heydrich. By the end of the Russian campaign about a million had been killed. The Yad Vashem account continues:

> Killing "operations" were carried out according to a set routine. First a large hole or trench was dug, usually by the victims themselves. Then the Nazis lined up the victims on the edge of the hole and mowed them down with a volley of shots...
> As early as July 31st, 1941, Reichsmarschall Hermann Göring sent an order in writing to Heydrich

"to make preparations for the general solution (*die Gesamtlösung*) of the Jewish problem within the German sphere of influence in Europe". On January 20th, 1942, a conference held in Wannsee, a suburb of Berlin… presided over by Heydrich… co-ordinated the plans for the extermination of the Jews. Heydrich gave the figure of eleven million as the number of Jews included in the plan for the "Final Solution" of the Jewish problem. This figure seems to indicate that he believed additional territory would fall into Nazi hands, as the Jews of those areas were also included in the overall plan. The minutes of the Wannsee Conference state: "As a result of the war, the programme for Jewish emigration has been changed for one of sending Jews to the east, according to the wish of Hitler".

The euphemism, "sending to the east", is clarified by a report by Rudolf Höss, commander of Auschwitz, who explains that he designated and enlarged the camp at Auschwitz for the purpose of responding to Hitler's orders, given to him through Himmler, because "the existing extermination points in the east were inadequate for large-scale, long-term activity".

One of the ironies of the modern world, with its multi-faceted progress, is the way in which new technological inventions, with their enormous potential for improving the lot of mankind, can contribute to ever more sophisticated acts of perversion and sadism, which undermine the very civilisation that produced them. It is difficult to imagine the Nazis carrying out their vast plan of genocide without the invention of the railways. Trainloads of up to a thousand Jews, crammed into cattle trucks, were brought to death camps from all over Europe. Michael Brown, in his book *Our Hands are Stained with Blood*, evokes the horrors of the journey: locked doors, no food, no water, very little air; "hour after hour the train rattles on; four endless days and four endless nights." He does not say where such a long journey began, but it may have been Western Europe, very likely France, where at Drancy, five kilometres north-east of Paris, the Nazis had an internment and transit camp for Jews from 1941 to 1944. Reitlinger describes the scene in the summer of 1942:

> 6,900 were collected at the Vélodrome d'Hiver, including all the children. It took five days to empty the Vélodrome d'Hiver. To pen people like cattle for days on end without food or water, without any of the comforts of existence and sometimes without a shred of clothing, had been the practice of the German police in Poland for the past four months and in Russia for the past year. The ordeal... was now repeated in the most civilised city in the world... no water except from a single street hydrant... ten latrines for 6,900 people...

Then Adolf Eichmann, head of the SS (and father of three small children) gave orders to send all the children (4,501 of them) to the "General Government", i.e. to Auschwitz in Poland. "No attendants went with the children in the sealed box cars, filled at that time with the old, the sick and the dying". When the children panicked and refused to leave the building, the gendarmes were called, who "carried the children in their arms, screaming with terror". Twenty-five of the children, aged between two and four, died on the journey.

In his book *Our Hands are Stained with Blood*, Brown asks how these things could happen in Christian Europe. He quotes Eliezer Berkovits' reference to "the moral bankruptcy of Christian civilisation" and his further observation:

After nineteen centuries of Christianity, the extermination of six million Jews, among them one-and-a-half million children, carried out in cold blood in the very heart of Christian Europe, encouraged by the criminal silence of virtually all Christendom, including that of an infallible Holy Father in Rome, was the natural culmination of this bankruptcy.

A brighter note in all this degradation is struck by Philippe Boegner's book, *Ici on a aimé les juifs* (Here we loved the Jews). He too tells of the horror of the "Vel d'Hiv" at Drancy, personally witnessed by a social worker and related by her to her friend Mme Dunan; but the book as a whole is the authentic story of the village of Chambon-sur-Lignon, in the Haute-Loire, where the entire population of sincere, Bible-reading Christians, led by a courageous pastor, and deeply conscious of their persecuted Huguenot forbears, welcomed and hid thousands of Jews and organised hundreds of escapes.

In France as a whole, and particularly in Vichy France, which the Germans occupied only after the Allied invasion of North Africa in 1942, the policy of rounding up Jews never worked fully, for French officials regarded French Jews as French first, whereas in Germany the view was becoming widespread that German Jews were not truly German. And part of Vichy France, in the south-east, was occupied by the Italians, who had a reputation of humanity towards the Jews, and helped many to escape into Italy. Holland was a different story, as Corrie Ten Boom notes with shame in her book *The Hiding Place*. She notes the increasing victimisation of Jews: their exclusion from public places and shops, the compulsory wearing of the yellow star, and the growing number who just disappeared. But in the midst of this darkness, there were lights that shone the more brightly, as Christian families like the

Ten Booms risked their lives, and indeed gave their lives, to shelter and protect their Jewish fellow-citizens.

Mention must be made furthermore of those two bright beacons of courage and compassion: Raoul Wallenberg and Oskar Schindler. Wallenberg came from a Lutheran family in Stockholm, Sweden. During the last winter of the war, he was sent to Budapest, capital of Hungary, by King Gustav V to negotiate the emigration of Jews. Thousands were being rounded up for deportation, or slaughtered by the "Arrow Cross" Hungarian fascists, as barbarous as their Nazi commanders, hanging their victims from lamp-posts before throwing their bodies into the Danube. Having worked in Palestine, and been deeply affected by stories of anti-semitic persecution told by refugees, Wallenberg negotiated tirelessly, taking advantage of the neutral status of his country; and with great courage personally arranged food and shelter or, where possible, Swedish passports. Threatened with being shot himself by Eichmann, he nevertheless saved the lives of thousands. In the end he sacrificed his own life, not to the Nazis, but to the invading Russians, in 1945. With permission to present his plan for helping the Jewish population to Marshall Malinovsky, he set off with an escort of Red Army soldiers, and was never seen again. Rumour suggested that the Soviet authorities could not believe that a capitalist Christian would risk his life just to save Jews; he must be an American spy. It is not surprising that one of the streets in central Budapest today bears his name.

Schindler was a German from Sudetenland, who came to Poland, after its occupation by Germany, to take over a factory in Cracow. A skilled businessman, and helped by a plentiful supply of Jewish labour, he quickly expanded the business. By the end of 1942, almost eight hundred men and women worked for him. Whilst outwardly cultivating cordial relations with the Nazi officers, he quietly did all he could to protect his Jewish workers, altering their documents to show that they were not too old or too young to work, amending their qualifications to show them as valuable manual workers for the war effort. He had the workers installed in a camp nearer the factory, officially to save working time, but also so that he could more easily reach them with food and medicines. Finally, when that camp was closed, he managed to obtain authorisation to set up a factory in Sudetenland and to transfer seven hundred men and three hundred women to it. Almost all of them survived until the 1945 liberation. The world has learned of his remarkable achievement through the film, "Schindler's List". When he died, he was buried in Jerusalem and a tree planted in his honour in the Avenue of the Righteous, by order of the Israeli government.

While all this was going on, the fate of Eva Baumann was unknown to the outside world. Her sister Hanna, writing a statement in 1955, says that Eva worked as assistant director of a Jewish old people's home in Berkaerstrasse, in Berlin-Schmargendorf. "Because the National Socialists had come to power, she could not find employment appropriate to her abilities, but had to take care of herself and the child." Hanna adds that her nephew Thomas was born in a hospital in Berlin, whose name and address she does not know; that he was placed in a children's home, and that her sister is dead, having been deported. Hanna must have learned of her sister's fate through Jewish contacts after the war in London and Berlin, but would have no detailed information. No wonder Tom has no recollections of his mother! He does recollect, however, that he was happy and well treated in the orphanages, enjoying the care of adults and the company of other children; not much contact with the outside world, but aware of the adults' anxiety and fear.

Hitler's "final solution". Map from *Holocaust Maps and Photographs, a visual narrative*, by Martin Gilbert; Fifth (Holocaust Educational Trust) Edition, London, 1998. Used with permission.

Chapter 12

God or Mammon

When he reached the age of forty, as Tom himself puts it, God spoke to him through his wife Judy. By this time (1972) he had managed to buy the freeholds of most of his properties, including the living accommodation over the shops. But now God intervened, to "heal his attitude to money", as his friend Jim Wilkinson would say. Tom was overworking, with no time for his family or church. In Tom's words, "God was in the background and Mammon was in the forefront". Judy quoted the words of Jesus: "Seek ye first the kingdom of God and his righteousness, and all these things shall be added unto you". So they decided to sell all the bakery shops; but this didn't work out as they expected. These shops represented a substantial commerce (using ten tons of flour a week) and all the big combines (Spillers, Rank, Weston, Allied Bakeries) showed interest; but Tom refused to sell to them because that would have meant closing the bakeries (attached to the bakery shops) and laying off a workforce of about fifty people. Tom had always believed in the importance of honesty and integrity in dealing with people who worked for him. Having worked himself in several businesses, where relationships were not always good, he determined that he would treat his employees as part of the family, paying them a decent wage, never asking them to undertake jobs that he would not do himself; he would work with them to make sure procedures were understood and then say, "You do it my way"! In the end he sold all seven businesses to a friend, who undertook to keep all the workforce, while Tom kept a financial interest as a consultant for ten years. He then sold the other businesses, except four launderettes; which brought an income to give living expenses and educate their three children in private schools. (Judy's father had also set up a trust fund to help with his grandchildren's education, but when he died he left his money to his third wife.) The actual freehold properties of the shops were not sold, except the residential parts (above the shops), and still brought an income for Tom and Judy's substantial living expenses many years later.

From 1972 onwards, Tom and Judy began to pray in earnest that God would show them what he wanted them to do, perhaps full time. The seeds of a plan began to germinate, to open a Christian centre. They placed a regular order for "Country Life", the magazine that devotes twenty pages each week to country houses and estates that are for sale. Between 1972 and 1977 they travelled all over the country, looking at country estates, at the rate of about one per month. They were attracted to a place in Shropshire, called Whitton Court, near Ludlow, with stables that might be converted, but they could not sell their businesses and houses, so were unable to proceed; a big blow that made them stop looking for the time being. Tom believes now that God was teaching them a lesson. He became an elder of the local Brethren church at Victoria Road, Wandsworth, near Wimbledon, and also ran the children's work and was involved in youth clubs and in practical community work organised by the church to help people in need. For seven years he took on the job of reading the notices, which gave him a new confidence to speak in public.

In the 1980s they began again to look for a suitable Christian centre, but because of their age, they decided it should be self-catering. And in 1984 "Country Life" advertised a place called "Elm House" at Redmire, near Leyburn, in North Yorkshire. It was a private house, but with the possibility of planning permission to change into a leisure centre or hotel. It had seventeen self-catering accommodations (so not needing a lot of staff); eight "lodges" and nine stone cottages around the court yard. Tom and Judy waited and prayed, for three months, then rang to see if it was still available. In September 1984 they went to look round, and felt sure that God was in their plans. They brought the family to see it. Philip agreed to come and take over the business side. They made a "take it or leave it" offer to the selling agent, who in effect accepted in a letter the next day, officially "in a fortnight". They were now committed to buying what they could not afford. Tom was given a year (October 1st 1984 to October 1st 1985) to pay the full price. He would have to sell his large family house in Wimbledon and four of his shops. A member of the Brethren church bought the house. One freehold flat was sold to its tenant. The shops were all sold by personal word-of-mouth contacts. All the money was available by the required date.

A big programme of redevelopment was started at Elm House, paid for by selling off properties in London: flats and shops. The first priority was to provide a conference centre for Christian groups, with seating for a hundred people and sleeping accommodation in the holiday cottages and lodges. A farm building was converted: the conference hall was downstairs with kitchens and toilet block; and upstairs a large private holiday accommodation with three bedrooms. Then central heating was installed for the first time in all the cottages and lodges and the old central heating in the main house was renewed. All the properties were re-equipped and refurnished. In 1987 four new lodges were built, sleeping five in each. They could now sleep over a hundred people on the site. So Tom sank a new bore hole, 200 feet down, supplying a holding tank of 6,000 gallons, with equipment to European Community standards. The total spent on Elm House estate from 1985 to 1996 was approximately half a million (£500,000).

Tom and Judy were now residents of the village of Redmire, mentioned in the Domesday Book of 1086, and already a village or settlement hundreds of years before that. It is set in one of the most beautiful of the Yorkshire dales, about half a mile north of the River Ure. For many years it was known as a lead-mining "town". Isabelle McGregor, in her book on Redmire's history, describes how at the time of the census in 1801 there was full employment for the growing population (320), as for the neighbouring village of Castle Bolton, because of the need of lead in the Napoleonic wars. After Waterloo (1815), work declined and many people left to find work in the towns of Lancashire or West Yorkshire or even in America. Today, at the end of the twentieth century, the population of Redmire is less than three hundred. The brochure that advertises Elm House as a holiday centre explains that it was originally a mediaeval manor house, complete with its own blacksmiths and joinering shops. In the seventeenth century, the then owners, the Other family, moved up to Elm House from Redmire village and several generations of the family lived there until 1972.

Nearby Castle Bolton takes its name from the castle built at the end of the fourteenth century by Sir Richard Scrope of Bolton, lord of the manor of Redmire. Eventually his descendants, or those who married into the family, were created Dukes of Bolton, and then in the eighteenth century, the first Baron Bolton. Much of the land in the area is still owned by Lord Bolton, and Bolton

Castle is an imposing monument on the skyline to the west of Redmire.

By far the oldest building in the village is Redmire Church, dating from about 1150, and proud of its well-preserved Norman doorway, with typical stone seats outside, where, so the publicity tells us, the sexton used to sit on Midsummer Eve and saw the ghosts of people who were to die within the next year.

The church at Redmire, of course, predates the Reformation, and so has survived many changes. It used to have a low, shuttered window in the south wall, to enable the priest to hear confessions from people kneeling on the grass outside. Such windows were blocked up on the orders of King Henry VIII. Of particular interest to Tom and Judy is a memorial to Thomas Other, whose family lived at Elm House from when it was built about 1690, for nearly three hundred years. From the church, Elm House can be seen across the fields.

From their first arrival in Redmire, Tom and Judy began a characteristically enthusiastic involvement both in financial commitments and in the fellowship and work of the Church. With the help of a £360,000 bank loan in 1988, they bought Briar Farm, whose land adjoined Elm House. It had once been part of the 11,000 acres of Elm House estate, whereas most of the other farms in the area are owned by Lord Bolton, whose estate also includes Bolton Castle and most of the village of Castle Bolton. To pay off the debt, Tom sold a substantial area of land, reaching right down to the River Ure. He also "did a swop" with Lord Bolton, who took some of the woodland from Briar Farm in exchange for land adjoining Elm House that Tom wanted to give enhanced privacy to the estate. Lord Bolton wanted the woodland for visitors who come and pay £2,000 a day for pheasant shooting. Tom sold a freehold shop in London for £250,000 and cleared the debt on the farm by the end of 1989. He and Judy let the land out to a farmer. The former farm house, a large, five-bedroomed house, is also rented out. Tom further bought a building site next to the farm and the house next door but one, although it needed large-scale renovation, to settle a problem of disputed land. On the building site, six houses were built for sale, with a further development of eight houses, in co-operation with Harewood housing society, to provide affordable homes for renting locally, and seven stone barns to be converted into two-, three- or four-bedroomed houses, also for renting.

In the midst of all this activity, they did not lose sight of the purpose of Elm House itself. It had two aspects: the commercial type of business which the Walters took over, with a list of charges for visitors during the tourist season; and the need to do something out of season, which tied in with Judy's vision for a conference centre, taking groups at weekends from churches and Christian organisations. These groups were not charged a fixed rate, but asked to give prayerful thought to expenses and contribute as they thought fit. This proved very interesting, says Tom (as an insight into human nature, even Christian human nature!): occasionally a group would pay nothing at all! On the whole the poorer churches were the most generous.

They were booked up solid for two years, so they decided to extend the voluntary charges system during the school holidays in July and August (which meant they lost their normal income for those months; they did, however, keep the normal system with fixed charges over Christmas and New Year). The Christian holidays were advertised in the Christian press and were always fully booked all July and August and every weekend in winter.

Throughout the holiday season (Easter to October) Christian meetings were held in Elm House: a Bible Study on one or two weekday evenings and a Sunday evening meeting when a local speaker would be invited, with a topic such as "What God has done in my life". These meetings were often supported, not only by the holiday visitors, but by people from local Christian fellowships in the Dales. However, Tom and Judy were anxious to avoid creating an exclusive Christian enclave that had no contact with the traditional Christian worship that was already part of Redmire village life; so they were only too pleased to receive a visit, soon after their arrival in 1985, from one of the church wardens, and to accept an invitation to join the members of Redmire church in their Sunday morning worship.

Last, but not least, there was another group to which Tom and Judy gave enthusiastic support, without which no picture of their Christian fellowship would be complete. Before they ever came to Yorkshire, Judy knew of a church called "Hollybush", which had featured on BBC Television's "Songs of Praise". Hollybush Christian Fellowship was the inspiration of Jim Wilkinson, or as he would prefer to put it, an inspiration to him from the Holy Spirit, to buy Hollybush Farm, near Northallerton, and form a new fellowship and Gospel outreach, free from the shackles of any denomination's tradition. He tells how it all happened in his book, *Miracle Valley*, published in 1984, the year that Tom and Judy bought Elm House. On one of their visits to the house, before they took over in 1985, they decided to travel the twenty-eight miles from Redmire, to try out Hollybush, and at once felt that here was a fellowship where they would feel at home. They have given it loyal support ever since, sharing particularly in its main gathering for worship and Bible teaching on Friday evenings. Their part in its Sunday activities is of course limited, because of commitments at Redmire Church and at Elm House.

Elm House.

The farm building converted into a conference centre, in the grounds of Elm House.

Some of the holiday lodges at Elm House.

The notice board at the entrance to Hollybush Christian Fellowship.

The Church of St Mary the Virgin, Redmire.

Chapter 13

The road to Auschwitz

One day the telephone rang at Elm House. Tom answered it. "This is Tyne Tees Television. We should like to do a programme about your life story." Tom hung up; thought it was a hoax; dismissed it from his mind. But it wasn't a hoax. Someone who had been to Elm House — a certain Will Crossley who had visited on several occasions — and heard Tom at one of the evening meetings speaking about his German Jewish background and last-minute escape from the Nazis, had contacted the television company with the suggestion that here was a story worth telling. They rang again, arranged to visit in March 1994, and asked permission to do research on Tom's background in Britain, Germany, Israel and the USA, with a view to making a television programme. Tom gave permission, and papers, to the Tyne Tees representative, Mark Robinson, who came with a microphone for informal chats, over a period of three months; after which he declared that there was enough material for a programme, but that it would cost a lot more than they had originally expected, so they would ask Yorkshire Television for help. This they did and Yorkshire agreed to share the cost. At this stage Tom was not told of all the research that they had already undertaken, but he was asked if he had any questions. "Yes," he said, "Why me?" (for the TV programme, out of so many Jews who had suffered). The answer was, because of the distance travelled, from a helpless Jewish child refugee to a prosperous Christian businessman.

A television team of eight spent four days at Elm House (16th to 19th August 1994), filming from 8 a.m. to 8 p.m. each day. They then asked Tom if he and Judy would be willing to go to Germany in two weeks' time, for four days, without knowing what was in store for them. They said they would; flew to Berlin, where six rooms had been booked at the prestigious Radisson Plaza Hotel, at £300 per night per room. Tom and Judy were introduced to Regine Wosnitza, a Berlin journalist, who, unknown to them, had been busy investigating on their behalf. On the first day they drove out to Altlandsberg, a picturesque little town in Brandenburg, about half an hour's drive east of Berlin. Regine led the way to an empty house, a dusty, dirty, cobwebby building; and Tom received his first shock of the visit when she quietly told him, "This is the house where you were born". She had checked with local registers and found the very building where Tom was brought into the world. The building, though empty at the time of their visit, was being renovated as an old people's home.

The next day was spent looking at the Jewish quarter in Berlin, with its newly rebuilt synagogue; then day three took them to the south-west side of the city, to an imposing building on the corner of Berkaerstrasse and Hohenzollerndamm, the main street leading from the city centre and Nürnbergerplatz, where Ludwig Bowman used to work before his retirement to Bavaria, and where his children were brought up. So Eva, Tom's mother, would have known the area well. It was to this building that she came with her baby in 1933, as assistant director of the well-equipped old people's home, opened only two years before, with accommodation for 180 people, its own synagogue seating 300, a roof garden, a prayer room on the third floor reached by a lift, day rooms on every floor, and spacious gardens covering about two acres of land. The building was designed by the architect Alexander Beer (same surname as Tom's great-grandfather who became Philip Bowman in America!), who wrote in the *Gemeindeblatt* (newsletter):

> The house will be remembered in the history of our community as a memorial to the generous willingness for sacrifice, with which the current generation honoured old age in times of hardship; and will visibly express their sympathy with those companions in faith who bore a hard lot.

Today the building houses the geriatric department of a council hospital. The Tyne Tees television programme commented that had Eva Baumann, Tom's mother, been still living at the time of his visit, she would have been the same age as a number of its present-day residents. A plaque on the wall ensures that the events of the Nazi régime are not forgotten:

> This house was built in 1930 as an old people's home for the Jewish community in Berlin by the architect Alexander Beer, 10.9.1873 — 8.5.1944. In 1941 it was confiscated by the SS; the last inhabitants and the nursing staff were deported and killed in concentration camps.
>
> Alexander Beer was deported to the concentration camp in Theresienstadt in 1943 and killed there on 8.5.1944.

It seems likely that Thomas lived with his mother in this splendid, but beleaguered, building until 1936. Then Eva's already desperate plight took an unbelievable turn for the worse. In February of that year she had to appear before a court in Bavaria, in connection with a suit for maintenance that she had filed against the man whom she claimed had fathered her child. He had challenged her claim, and since the court had accepted his challenge and rejected her claim, she was sentenced to one year and four months' imprisonment for perjury. The surviving extract from police records in the Berlin legal department dates from 1955, by which time the first names and family names of both Eva's parents are said to be *unbekannt* (unknown). Their records had long since been removed from the registry office by the Nazis.

Little Thomas, not yet four years old, was placed in an orphanage (destroyed later in the wartime bombing), on the other side of the city: the Reichenheimsche orphanage, run by the Jewish community since its foundation in 1872 with money donated by Moritz and Sara Reichenheim. The daughter of a former director, Elisabeth Feist-Hirsch, describes, in an essay published in 1970, how her father ran the home from 1906 to 1935. The discipline was traditional: boys and girls were strictly separated and paraded each morning before being allowed into breakfast. Dr Feist "did not refrain from using the stick sometimes", especially for lies, bad marks, stealing or fights. On the other hand, he "had a lot of understanding for, and interest in, young people and helped them whenever he could". The festivals of the Jewish year were strictly observed, also the great Day of Atonement (*Yom Kippur*). All the children looked forward to the Feast of Tabernacles (*Sukkot*), when "a hut made of leaves was constructed", and especially enjoyed the impressive beauty and symbolism of Passover and Hanukkah.

Dr Feist's daughter also tells how the officer at the police station next door did his best to offer help and protection when Hitler came to power, in return for shelter that he had been given when he fled from revolutionary violence after the first world war. However, it was becoming impossible for anyone to guarantee safety for Jews in Berlin, and Eva was one of many parents who determined to send their children away to places where they might be overlooked. She had been released from prison in February 1937, but a year later arranged for Thomas to move to a children's home at Herrlingen, near Ulm, in South Germany. Here he stayed until, at the beginning of 1939, the head of the home decided that he himself would move to England, presumably when he received orders to close the home down. By this time the "British Society for the Propagation of the Gospel among the Jews" had already alerted people in England to the urgent need for foster parents for Jewish children and, as we have already seen, the secretary of that society was already in correspondence with Mr and Mrs Walters regarding their wish to adopt. In the meantime, on the 21st April, four days before the British Home Office gave permission, Thomas was transferred to a third orphanage, the *Wilhelmspflege*, in Esslingen, near Stuttgart. This home had a very good reputation for enlightened, liberal education. The headmaster, Theodor Rothschild (not related to the English branch) "tried to give the feeling of a great family to the children. The independence of the children was trained very early on. Every child was responsible for a small task that he liked and was good at carrying out".

Until 1938 the older children had also been given vocational training. Then, on *Kristallnacht* (9th/10th November 1938) the home was destroyed and looted. But the Rothschilds were successful in gaining permission to re-open in February 1939, two months before Tom's arrival. His departure to England was two months before the home was finally confiscated by the Gestapo, and turned into a hospital. On the 8th September 1939, Rothschild wrote a letter to the school authorities stating, "Our children are accommodated in families and there is no possibility of assembling them again. Our school therefore does not exist any longer for the time being".

It is not quite clear how long Eva Baumann kept her employment at the Berkaerstrasse home, but she had already left before its residents and nursing staff were deported in 1941. As for her little boy, so for herself, she had so far managed to keep one step ahead of the Gestapo and had moved to another old people's home in Schönhauser Allee. Her name is listed on a document issued by the Association of Jews in Germany, dated 1st September 1941. The entry on her reads: "Eva Sara Baumann — single — no child — servant" and gives her salary (grade VII) as 94,30 Reichsmarks gross, RM 27,28 net (after deduction for board and expenses). This building was in former East Berlin, next to a Jewish cemetery; and today houses a police station.

There were two more places to see, on day four: the site of a former impressive building in Große Hamburger Straße, and Grunewald railway station. The building is no longer there; it was bombed and destroyed by the Allies at the end of the war. It was an old people's home for fairly well-to-do people and had a very good reputation. Opened in 1874, it celebrated its fiftieth anniversary in 1924 with a visit from the Empress, who presented a portrait of her husband, the Kaiser, then living in exile in Holland. After 1933, when Hitler came to power, everything changed. In that same year Rabbi Riesenburger took office as leader of the synagogue. He later recorded his memories in a book entitled *Das Licht verlöschte nicht* (the light did not go out). Regine tells in the TV programme, whilst in Berlin with Tom and Judy, how the rabbi was told to leave the synagogue in the middle of a festival celebration. She then quotes the following passage from his book:

> The Gestapo moved into this building, and so the house was turned into the infamous *Judenlager* (Jew camp). At this place, that had been erected for the preservation of life, now thousands of people were stored as a preparation for extermination and death. Like a prison, the building was equipped with bars; guards were posted on the street and at the main gate; and huge spotlights were installed at the front and the back to prevent any escapes during the night. Herded together like cattle, lying on the floor, old and young people, men, women, children and even babies had to await the moment of their final barbaric deportation... an endless trail of outlaws on the big and dark street of death. All this took place night by night under the horror of darkness.

At the end of October 1942 the chief of the headquarters of Jewish emigration in Vienna was ordered to Berlin to sort out corruption in the Berlin Gestapo. One of his first acts was to empty the Große Hamburger Straße building of all its furniture, leaving the inmates with nothing but mattresses.

It was to this building that Eva was ordered to report, to be deported "to the east". Before deportation each person had to fill in and sign a property declaration (*Vermögenserklärung*). The purpose of such apparently pointless bureaucracy was evidently to enable the Nazis to confiscate Jewish property more easily and quickly. In view of the terrible destination that lay ahead, the last sentence above the victim's signature is particularly callous: "I am aware that false or incomplete statements will be punished".

Eva filled in her form on the 5th December 1942. Unbeknown to Tom, but with his authority to conduct research for the television company, Regine had found the document; and it was a poignant moment when she produced it and showed it to Tom as he and Judy sat with her on a seat facing the site of the former infamous building, during their 1994 visit. There was his mother's own signature, Eva Sara Baumann. Every Jewish woman in Hitler's Germany had to add the name Sara to her signature, for instant identification. Eva's real second name was Felicitas, which means happy or fortunate! On the form itself, all sections are blank, for Eva had no possessions, with two exceptions: the section on financial assets give details of a bank account, containing nothing; and in the section about children, in answer to the question, "What family dependants have already emigrated? Where to?", Eva has written, "Thomas Israel Baumann, *abgewandert* (emigrated elsewhere)". Israel was a compulsory addition to the name of all Jewish males. Eva either does not know, or is not prepared to say, to which country Thomas has gone, but here is clear evidence that, before she went to her death, she knew that her little boy was safely out of the country. She was deported four days later from Grunewald station, on the western outskirts of Berlin, which the *Ost-Transport* used to avoid the notice of the city centre population. This was Tom and Judy's final visit with the television crew. They saw the marshalling yards where the cattle-trucks came and went. Regine had also discovered other documents: one states that all Eva's property was confiscated on the 1st October 1942; on the 29th December 1942 the Deutsche Bank returned her savings account book to the Jewish Community in Oranienburger Strasse; on the 27th November 1944 the bank informed the tax office that they had transferred RM 105,50 from Eva's bank account to the authorities and that they regarded their dealings with the owner of the account as closed! Regine ascertained that the 24th *Ost-Transport* (which deported Eva on the 9th December 1942) took 1060 men, women and children to Auschwitz. On arrival 137 men (with numbers 81263 to 81399) and 25 women (with numbers 26621 to 26645) were selected to work in the prison camp; the remaining 898 people were killed straight away in the gas chambers. Eva is listed as *verschollen* (presumed dead) in the *Gedenkbuch* (Memorial Book) of victims of persecution of the Jews under the National Socialist Tyranny in Germany, 1933-1945.

A document which Regine received (in Polish) from the archives in Auschwitz, states that of the more than a million who died there, 50,335 came from Berlin. Remarkably, 178 people survived deportation to Auschwitz. One of them, Anneliese-Ora Borinski (deported in 1943), wrote of the horrors of those days in her *Erinnerungen* (Memoirs) *1940-1943*, published in 1970. She tells of prayers on Sunday evening before a very early Monday morning departure on waiting trucks, transfer at the station to cattle-wagons, with straw on the floor and doors locked from the outside. Through the small window, during the journey, they sometimes see groups of people working, some wearing the yellow star, many in the uniform of prisoners of war. "We ask them for the direction, the possible destination of our train. They shrug their shoulders. One of them points to the sky. We do not understand anything." Then suddenly they arrive at a place called Auschwitz. They are ordered off the train, men separated from the women, told that they and their luggage will all be together again soon. They march in ranks, flanked by SS guards. "It's not far. We suddenly see barbed wire in front of us, barbed wire everywhere. We see a huge gate in front of us, SS guards with dragging, snorting and barking dogs, and through this gate we walk in. Very upright, and without realising, that at that moment we have entered Auschwitz, the concentration and extermination camp."

No words can explain the enormity of these crimes against humanity. "Why did it all happen?" Tom asks in the television programme, and then adds, "People say to me, 'Why does God allow all this?' I have to say to them, God doesn't allow it; it's not God's fault; this is unfortunately what man has done". Which still leaves us disturbed at the potential for depravity and contradiction in the human soul and the manipulative power of evil dictators. It is said that some of the guards at Auschwitz showed their concern for bird life by putting up nesting boxes, and we have to imagine them going home from their daily supervision of torture and death to the comfort and relaxation of their own families. We do not know if Eva had the will or the strength to say the Shema' with her last breath, but we do know, from a survivor, that the tormented, despairing prisoners on Christmas Eve, as they lay starving and hopeless, heard the guards singing hymns and Christmas carols, so declaring their belief, in theory at least, in the One who came to bring glory to God and peace on earth!

The district of Berlin where Eva, Tom's mother, grew up.

The Old People's Home in Große Hamburger Straße which was requisitioned by the Gestapo, and from which building Eva was deported.

The house in Atlandsberg where Tom was born.

Ich erkläre ausdrücklich, daß ich meine vorstehenden Angaben nach bestem Wissen gemacht und dabei insbesondere keinerlei Vermögenswerte verschwiegen habe. Ich versichere weiterhin, außer für meine Ehefrau und meine Kinder, deren Vermögen ich besonders angegeben habe, für andere Personen nur solche Vermögenswerte zu verwalten oder in Gewahrsam zu haben, die von mir ausdrücklich in dieser Vermögenserklärung (falls nicht anderweitig, in der letzten Spalte unter Verschiedenes) als fremde bezeichnet worden sind. Ich bin mir bewußt, daß falsche oder unvollständige Angaben geahndet werden.

Berlin, den 5. Dez. 42

Eva Sara Baumann
(Unterschrift)

Eva's signature at the end of the property declaration, written just before her deportation.

Welche Familienangehörigen sind schon ausgewandert? Wohin?

Thomas Israel Baumann, ausgewandert

Eva's declaration about the existence and whereabouts of "Thomas Israel Baumann".

Chapter 14

One foundation

Important as it is, the background of Tom's early life and his mother's tragic death is not the whole story that Tyne Tees Television wanted to tell. Their film tells how the little Jewish boy became a Christian, under the influence of his adoptive mother, and though the television presentation of it is somewhat melodramatic, with a blinding light conversion redolent of Saul of Tarsus on the road to Damascus, nevertheless it gives the right impression of a decision taken that was to influence the rest of his life, and still shapes his motives and priorities fifty-five years later. For Tom, being a Christian does not mean that he has ceased to be a Jew, or that he has left one culture and joined another. He does not believe that all Jewish beliefs and practices are wrong and all beliefs and practices under a Christian umbrella are right. His loyalty is first and foremost to Jesus, the Messiah of the Jews and the Church's one foundation. His life is still based on the response he made as a boy to those words of the risen Lord Jesus in the Book of Revelation:

> *"I stand at the door and knock; if anyone hears my voice and opens the door, I will come in."*

How is this loyalty to be expressed in practice? First of all by being a Christian in the place where you live. Tom and

Judy believe strongly in being involved in the local community, and in giving support to the worship and witness of the local church. Services are held in Redmire Church on Sunday mornings, but only in alternate weeks. This is because Castle Bolton also has its own church building, and in recent years neither church has been considered large enough to operate independently, so that they have joined together as the parish of Bolton-cum-Redmire. Once a fortnight a service is held at Redmire and on the alternate Sunday mornings at Castle Bolton.

In 1991 Tom was invited to be a member of the parochial parish council. He accepted, but then came a shock: his nomination was opposed, because he was not officially a member of the church (this was news to Tom!). He was not a member of the church, he was told, because he had not been baptised or confirmed. He explained that he had indeed been baptised, as a believer, though not as an infant. The vicar, the Revd Martin Brown, checked in the book of canon law and found that believer's baptism could be accepted as valid (surely the New Testament could have told them that!), but there was still the question of confirmation. Tom, ever positive, agreed to be confirmed. If this was the Church of England's way of declaring your faith, so be it! He was confirmed by Bishop Michael Menham, Bishop of Knaresborough, on the 12th July 1991 and soon afterwards accepted as a member of the P.C.C. and eventually also of the Deanery Synod.

Since March 1996, the vicar of Bolton-cum-Redmire has been the Revd Susan Whitehouse. She is also vicar of Aysgarth, about five miles away (famous for its picturesque waterfalls), so has to hurry away after the Redmire and Castle Bolton services, to take a second Sunday morning service with the Aysgarth church. Tom and Judy feel at home in the church and appreciate the lead given by Susan. The Sunday morning service is traditional, with Bible readings from the Old and New Testaments, following the annual lectionary. Susan's sermon is a clear, non-repetitive and thought-provoking exposition of a Bible passage; it lasts seven minutes. The service lasts about an hour. Special extra services are held at Christmas and Easter and a six-week Lent course offers teaching and fellowship in people's homes or the church or the village hall. And occasionally the church takes to the streets, or at least to the village green, with singing led by a brass ensemble making "a joyful noise", and light refreshments served afterwards.

For centuries the centre of the village community has been the parish church. But the history of Methodism is also important. John Wesley first came to the area as a friend of the Rector of Wensley, the Revd John Clayton. He preached at both Redmire and Castle Bolton on the 24th May 1744. At that time he was himself an Anglican clergyman, wanting to revive the Church of England, rather than start a new denomination of "Methodists". It is recorded that he visited again in 1774 and preached under the old oak tree which is still there for everyone to see. Early in the nineteenth century a Methodist chapel was built, was later enlarged and a gallery added, and for many years there was a flourishing Methodist Sunday School, but by the last quarter of the twentieth century numbers had declined, the small congregation amalgamated with Castle Bolton Methodist Chapel and the Redmire building became the village hall. Tom keeps in touch with the Methodists too and supports the prayer meeting held once a month in one of their churches. He has considered allowing his name to go on the list of Methodist lay preachers, but the thought of travelling around the North Yorkshire dales to preaching engagements, along winding country lanes in bad weather on dark winter nights, has so far persuaded his better judgement that he has enough on his plate already.

The different types of churches in North Yorkshire give ample illustration of the variety of worship that British churches and fellowships offer at the end of the twentieth century. Tom and Judy are happy to find Christian brothers and sisters in all sorts of traditions. They are at the same time challenged to discern what is important, indeed fundamental, to their faith, and what is merely tradition, or habit, or current fashion. Some churches teach that to arrange the precise format or length of a service beforehand is to inhibit the work of the Holy Spirit. Others believe that God works through careful planning and tradition. The Hollybush fellowship near Northallerton is an example of the former. The Anglican twin churches of Castle Bolton and Redmire would place emphasis on the latter. We may remember that the apostle Paul once preached till midnight (we don't know what time he started), then carried on talking until dawn, even after a young man had been overcome by sleep and fallen out of the upstairs window of the room where they were meeting! But it was a special occasion, charged with emotion because they did not expect ever to meet again. It was also Paul who wrote, "Let everything be done in a fitting and orderly way", and that was particularly in relation to confusion about the exercise of spiritual gifts, in the church at Corinth.

The Greek word for spiritual gifts in the New Testament is *charismata*, and this is the origin of the word "charismatic", which for some twenty years now has been popularly applied to a movement which has influenced all the main Christian denominations, as well as many independent fellowships and groups of churches. A dominant theme in their preaching and worship is an emphasis on the activity of the Holy Spirit; the need to be filled with the Spirit, baptised in the Spirit, even slain in the

Spirit. They believe in all the gifts that the Holy Spirit gives for edifying all the members of the church (as explained in Paul's letters to the Corinthians and Ephesians), but give special prominence to those conspicuous gifts which they believe the traditional churches have conspicuously neglected, such as speaking in tongues, physical healing and spontaneous announcements known as "prophecy" or "words of knowledge". 1 Corinthians chapter 12 lists some "gifts" of the Spirit: the word of wisdom, the word of knowledge, faith, gifts of healing, working of miracles, prophecy, discerning of spirits, tongues, the interpretation of tongues. Galatians chapter 5 lists some of the "fruit" of the Spirit: love, joy, peace, longsuffering, gentleness, goodness, faithfulness, meekness, self-control. Both charismatic churches and traditional churches believe in all these things, since they share a common respect for the Bible, but whilst the charismatics give prominence to the gifts, perhaps the traditionalists feel more at ease with the fruit.

Where does the Hollybush fellowship fit into all this? Jim Wilkinson explains how it came into existence, in his book, *Miracle Valley*. He is aware of the dangers of personal opinions or impressions being passed off as "prophecies" or "words of knowledge". In his own words, "Anyone could manipulate events to their advantage by claiming that 'God told me...'" None-the-less, *Miracle Valley* is the account of God's continuous guidance (and blessing, which is surely a confirmation of guidance), sometimes through circumstances, sometimes through the clear words of Scripture, but quite often through spontaneous revelations ("I suddenly knew"; "I just feel it in my spirit") or out-of-the blue prophecies ("Lend what thou hast"; "thou must not skimp"). Perhaps most startling of all, in Jim's book, is the way in which he chose his wife — already someone else's girlfriend, because in the middle of a church service when she was the soloist and he was the preacher, the Lord said to him, "That's the girl I've got for you"! (incidentally, an unusually modern turn of phrase; most of the messages received in "prophecies" seem to be in seventeenth-century English). Here, too, however, blessing has followed, in a happy marriage of over forty years.

Jim and his wife Cynthia believe that the Hollybush fellowship came into being as a result of a direct word from the Lord. Way back in March 1968, shortly after dismissing with a laugh a Christian friend's vision of buying a vast area of land for a Christian centre, Jim heard the Lord's voice as he drove past Hollybush Farm: "I want that place for my glory". The years since then have seen impressive results. The land was bought, meetings began in the farmhouse, then in a converted barn, and eventually in a large purpose-built building holding about 750 people. Meetings are held on Sundays at 10.30 and 6.30, each lasting up to two hours; but the main gathering of the fellowship is on Friday evenings at 7.30, for at least two hours. Well-known speakers are invited from all over Britain and even America, and many of the congregation travel long distances to be present. In addition to these weekly activities, members of the fellowship take services in other churches and speak at meetings in schools and colleges, prisons and old people's homes. Many of the members have gone overseas, to over twenty countries, as evangelists and to support with financial and practical help. The fellowship also sells thousands of tapes and videos of meetings held and addresses given at Hollybush. There is also a very busy letter writing activity, answering hundreds of letters from readers of the book, "Miracle Valley". And there are camps on the field for special weekends and a week-long summer camp, attended by many hundreds, who bring their own tents and caravans. 1997 was a special 25th anniversary camp, since these camps began in 1972. Each day's programme included prayer and Bible study meetings, youth meetings and children's meetings. The theme text of the week in 1997 was, "Where the Spirit of the Lord is, there is liberty".

Someone has written that you can tell whether a church is charismatic or traditional the moment you walk into the building. In a traditional church, people sit at the back first; latecomers have to go to the front. In a charismatic church, those who arrive first go to the front; others fill up the seats behind them, because everyone wants to play an active part in the worship. Another difference (with a risk of exaggeration) is in the style of the singing and musical accompaniment. In one it is sedate and dignified; in the other loud and fast. At Redmire, the organ is played carefully and professionally. At Hollybush there is a keyboard (or two?) and several other instruments; the musicians are expected to improvise, to be able to lead worship without a pre-arranged order of service. Jim writes of a snag that cropped up when the Fellowship was joined by a musician, a brass band player, who had been trained to play "from sheet music". He trusted God for a miracle, to enable him to play by ear.

In the end, of course, it is not good singing that is the foundation of the church, even if "Methodism was born in song". It is what the church believes and teaches that makes the foundation. "No other foundation can anyone lay than that which is laid, which is Jesus Christ". So Jim Wilkinson was quite happy to be questioned about the teaching at Hollybush. First of all, the relationship with the established Christian denominations. Jim relates in his book how he and Cynthia came to sever their links with the Methodist church where they had spent years of happy service. Jim continues, "The Lord spoke directly to us through prophecy: '...do not affiliate yourselves to any one group, for I the Lord have brought you out of denominationalism'." Here then are some of the questions and answers:

Are you interdenominational?
Yes. Our speakers come from nearly all the main denominations. Our policy is to be friends with all without any links with one particular denomination.
Does your church belong to any federation?
Yes, the Evangelical Alliance.
Are you the pastor of the church?
Yes.
You have a "leadership team"; do you have elders?
We have one elder at present, and are planning to have another two.
Who will appoint them?
I shall appoint one, and all the members will vote to appoint the other one.
Do you teach a baptism of the Holy Spirit?
Yes.
When does it take place?
Any time.
Why do you baptise by immersion (in the River Wiske, for example, as shown in the Tyne Tees Television programme)? Why do you not baptise infants?
We believe the Bible teaches that baptism is for believers only. We dedicate infants, but do not baptise them.
What do you think of the Church of England teaching and practice on these things?
We could regard their P.C.C. as roughly the equivalent of our elders. We think they are wrong to baptise infants.
Are you happy that Tom is a confirmed member of the Church of England and a member of the deanery

synod, as well as a member of your church?
Not really; (then, after a moment's pause) my spirit
is happy; my soul is not.

Jim then recognised that Tom was in an unusual situation
and wished him God's blessing, remembering that Paul was
ready to be "all things to all men", in order to win some.

In the Hollybush brochure of 1997, celebrating 25 years
of camp meetings, the beliefs of the fellowship are clearly
set out. They are in fact the beliefs of all the main Christian
denominations, including the Trinity, the deity of Jesus
Christ, his substitutionary death, his resurrection and
promise of return; the sinfulness of all men, salvation by
grace through faith; and the Bible as the ultimate authority
for faith and practice.

There have always been churches throughout the world
and throughout the centuries, whose ideal has been to
build upon this same foundation, though inevitably all
have fallen short of their ideals, and sometimes begun to
build "on the sand" instead of "on the rock". They have
failed to preach the gospel of Jesus Christ, or they have
failed to practise what they preached. And how often —
far too often — have they been suspicious of one another
or alienated by the way the message is presented! Not
everyone would feel at home with the style of Hollybush's
worship, even though they felt the presence of the Lord
and appreciated the message of the preacher. Even less
would they feel happy when people fell to the ground and
"laughed in the Spirit" in the manner of the "Toronto
blessing". Jim Wilkinson admits in his book: "We couldn't
point to any examples of the same thing taking place in the
Scriptures". Much easier to justify from the Scriptures is
the doctrine of assurance of salvation, though some
individual "testimonies" are more convincing than others.
"He who hears my word", said Jesus, and believes him

who sent me… shall not come into condemnation, but has passed from death to life". Tom Walters is aware that some of his friends in the Church of England are repelled by his dogmatic assertion that his sins have been forgiven and his place in heaven assured. And yet, they are happy to sing those very same certainties from the hymn book:

> Praise, my soul, the King of heaven…
> Ransomed, healed, restored, forgiven,
> Who like me his praise should sing?

Tom and Judy share this assurance. What about the members of their family, their two sons Stephen and Philip, and their daughter Jane? Have they built on the same foundation? What do they think of their family background and the things that they have been taught? Listen first to Judy's view of her children's upbringing: Jane, the eldest, "didn't take kindly to rules, but never had any big problems"; Stephen had "a time of questioning at university" and finished after two years. He did not join the Christian Union, but did find a church to go to, but with no welcome in people's homes. This must have been a disappointment to him, and a marked contrast to the welcome that students would have found in his parents' home. Philip "has always been very placid". Interestingly enough, all three have expressed agreement with their mother's assessment! And all three followed their parents' example of personal commitment to Jesus Christ as Saviour and Lord; Jane at the age of sixteen, at a camp run by the Brethren church at Victoria Hall; Stephen at the age of thirteen, at a "Crusader" camp in Bembridge; and Philip, at the same camp the year before, at the age of nine. Speaking more generally of their upbringing, Stephen saw his father as quite a good listener, but not very good at delegating. It was always a question of "Do it my way"!

And it had never occurred to Stephen, until questioned about it, that he had German-Jewish roots, although he knew his father had! He and his wife Jane live in Wandsworth (with their three children, Jenna, Abby and Joshua), where he is an elder at Westside Church, the Brethren church (with a new name) where his father was an elder twenty years ago. He believes that God's promises to Israel in the Old Testament are to be fulfilled in those who have accepted Jesus as Messiah, God's new people, Jews or Gentiles; with no special future for the nation of Israel. Philip, on the other hand, believes that in addition to his plans for the Church, God still has special blessings in store for Israel. Philip is a member of Brixton City Church, advertised as the "young people's church", led by the missionary organisation known as YWAM (Youth with a Mission). Founded in 1970, YWAM is an interdenominational mission. There are currently some 350 YWAM workers in Britain, helping churches with evangelism and youth and children's work; and urban teams with special responsibility for inner city areas, concerned with rehabilitation from drugs dependency, help for the homeless and those living by prostitution, caring for AIDS sufferers, or teaching computer skills to young people. There are also about 250 workers on long-term overseas missions, including the staffing of four "mercy ships", bringing health care and relief to the poorest peoples of the world, reclaiming desert land through water resource management, and creating projects to give employment skills to orphans. After training at the YWAM Bible College in Homestead Manor, Sussex, Philip spent two months on a YWAM project in India, and is now committed full time to the work of the Mission. His sister Jane, with her husband Terry and their three boys, Simeon, Nathan and Jacob, live at Leamington Spa, where they attend a URC church. It is near to where they live and they enjoy good fellowship, though Jane reflects that her children could miss out on an understanding of believer's baptism. And what about the six grandchildren's understanding of Tom's background? Do they know about his childhood or his mother's fate? The older ones do, for they have seen a video recording of the Tyne Tees television programme. No doubt the younger ones will see it in due course.

One more fellowship must be mentioned to complete the kaleidoscope of Tom and Judy's Christian contacts in North Yorkshire. In 1990 "United Christian Worship" was started in Leyburn, the nearest town to Redmire, by Helen and Bill Lee, with Anglican, Roman Catholic and Methodist churches holding a joint service on the first Sunday evening of each month. They also began a number of house-group Bible studies, once a fortnight. When this united worship began, Tom and Judy cancelled their meeting at Elm House on the first Sunday of the month, so that they could support the new venture. Helen Lee is a well-known writer and international speaker; her husband is a retired vicar. Their son is a full-time worker with the Universities' and Colleges' Christian Fellowship (UCCF). On one occasion, when Helen was the invited speaker at a meeting in the Elm House conference centre, she took the subject, "oaks of righteousness, a planting of the LORD", from Isaiah 61 verse 3, to show that, in spite of all the chaos in the world, God is at work and will not abandon those who trust him. She then told two light-hearted, but true stories, both giving food for thought in relation to today's Church and its foundations. The first was the story of a group of English young people giving out Christian literature in an eastern European country and being opposed by the local Orthodox priests. They were asked to appear before the head of the Orthodox Church and were ushered into his presence, not without some feelings of trepidation on their part. He began to speak: "Do you know John Stott?", he said, "do you know Jim Packer?" The young people were able to say that they knew them well and that the literature they were giving out was produced by the same organisation (IVP) that published the books that John Stott and Jim Packer wrote. The Orthodox leader had greatly appreciated the two men's Bible-based books. He gave the young people his enthusiastic blessing.

Helen told the second story after congratulating the chairman on his succinct introduction as he invited her to speak. It was the story of a meeting when Helen herself had been the second of two speakers. The first speaker was blind, and had a guide dog, but the congregation could not see the dog because of the high platform rail in the Methodist church. The chairman of that meeting was very verbose. When he was in full flow for the second time (between the two speakers), Helen leaned forward for her bag and the dog, thinking this was the signal to depart, stood up. "Sit!" said Helen sharply, and both dog and chairman did so immediately. "We were never asked again!" was Helen's husband's laconic comment.

Revd Susan Whitehouse, vicar of Bolton-cum-Redmire and Aysgarth; with Judy and Tom Walters.

The old oak tree at Redmire, where John Wesley preached in 1774.

Jim Wilkinson with Tom Walters at the Hollybush Fellowship.

All the family: Stephen, Josh, Jane (Stephen's wife), Philip, Judy, Nathan, Tom, Jane, Terry (Jane's husband), Simon; front row: Abby, Jake and Jenna.

Chapter 15

Elm House estate for sale

When Tom and Judy returned from holiday in February 1993, Philip told them that he had a calling from God to work full time as a missionary, but that he would stay for another two years before giving up his commitments at Elm House, in accordance with the promise he had made to his father that he would give two years' notice. At this time he was virtually running the office and jointly, with his parents, running the holiday business. Tom explains how they dealt with this new situation. First of all they prayed for guidance. Then they considered getting a manager in to replace Philip, but rejected the idea as possibly bringing future complications. They decided to have the estate valued by a national estate agent. The valuation was £1½ million, apart from the farm. Brochures and photographs were produced and, on the 1st October 1994, the estate was advertised for sale. Very quickly there was an enormous amount of interest. Quite soon a buyer was found for the whole estate; he asked if Tom and Judy could move out by Christmas. Their solicitor advised against the deal, so they rejected it. During the next twelve months, sixty-five people came to see the property.

It became clear that there were two types of prospective buyers: those who wanted the house only, and those who wanted the business but not the house. In September 1995

the agents decided on a dead-line date: a final offer by 1st
October 1995. They wrote again to the eight hundred
people who had had a brochure, in the hope of a "Dutch
auction", that is, accepting the highest of several bids. The
result was three offers, all of them unacceptable.

At the same time, one of the parties that had booked a
holiday at Elm House was a "Lydia Prayer Group" (taking
their name, no doubt, from Lydia in the Acts of the
Apostles, who met for prayer with other women in
Philippi). They were a group of women who had booked
for a conference, to pray for national needs. During their
stay, six of them, who knew that the estate was for sale,
came to the house and "buttonholed" Tom, saying that
God had spoken to them about Elm House. They gave
Tom and Judy a paper on which was written their
conviction that the estate must be sold only to people who
would continue to use it as a Christian centre. Tom and
Judy accepted this and withdrew the property from the
sale. They decided it would be a good idea to split the
estate into two: to sell the holiday business first. This
necessitated building a new access road and new fencing,
to make the holiday business self-contained, separate from
the house and the rest of the estate. Then, in November
1995, one member of the Lydia Prayer Group turned up
again. She was on holiday in her caravan in West Burton,
three or four miles from Redmire, still praying about the
future of Elm House. She felt that the Lord had a further
message for Tom. "You must advertise your business in
Christian magazines," she said. Tom and Judy agreed.
They advertised in *Alpha*, *Renewal* and *Parentwise* in
December 1995, January 1996 and February 1996. At the
same time, several of their friends at the Hollybush
Fellowship spoke to them through "prophecies", that is to
say, with the conviction that God was guiding their
thoughts. They believed that there would be five parts to

this guidance: 1) it would begin in January; 2) there would be four people; 3) there would be a red car; 4) the business would be taken over "when the apples fall"; 5) there would be guidance to a new place when Elm House was sold. Tom and Judy felt that God was at work, showing them the next step.

They were not disappointed. It just so happened that four people (two couples), working for the Church Pastoral Aid Society (CPAS), had been praying about a holiday complex, with lodges suitable for self-catering, a field and a conference centre. They had already established a trust, called the Jonas Trust, with a view to buying a property and putting their plan into action. On the evening of the 30th December 1995, the daughter of one of the couples went to bed with the *Alpha* magazine, saw the advert and took it straight away to her parents, who wrote the next day to ask for an interview. They prayed (Gideon-like) for three points of guidance: 1) that the vendors would be Christians; 2) that they would be flexible about time; 3) that they would be flexible about money. So it came about that four people came at the beginning of January and were very interested in the site and its facilities. They said they would ask their trustees to come and investigate. The trustees came in a red car. By March 1996, sixteen other potential buyers had come. Then someone offered to buy the whole estate, so Tom contacted the January four, met them in Warwick where they lived and worked, and made an agreement that by the 1st October 1996 they would take over the holiday business, buying the twelve lodges and the conference centre, with a large field; and renting the courtyard stone cottages. Half the money was to be paid on the 1st October 1996 and the other half, interest free, over the next two years.

The four members of the Jonas Trust were George and Jill Lihou, and Peter and Jennie Gallant. George used to be a primary school headteacher in London. At the time of setting up the Trust, he was working full time with the CPAS, responsible for training and resourcing children's leaders and running children's camps at Clymping, in Surrey. His wife, Jill, had worked as a nurse and been involved in caring for the elderly. The CPAS is advertised as being an evangelical Anglican mission agency, dedicated to resourcing the local church for mission. It has the largest church-based youth and children's work in the Anglican churches of the UK and Ireland. Peter Gallant was in senior management in a local government post and was also experienced, like George, in running children's camps. His wife, Jennie, was a primary school teacher.

While he was working with the children's camps, George explains, the Lord said to him, "Why only two weeks in the summer?" As the brochure puts it: "We believe that God has guided the Trust to develop part of the lovely Elm House Estate, at Redmire on the edge of the Yorkshire Dales National Park. Within 50 miles there are forty large towns including Newcastle, Gateshead, Middlesborough, York, Leeds, Bradford, Huddersfield and Blackburn. There are another thirty large towns within 75 miles". The introduction to the same leaflet states: "The Jonas Trust has been formed to provide facilities for differing groups and individuals to 'come away from it all' and discover what God can make possible in their lives". The priority in accepting bookings is "for younger children and for children and families who are most in need and least able to afford commercial rates". Disadvantaged families, carers, and others who would benefit from time away and the support offered by the Trust, are recommended by churches. A subsidy fund operates to enable those who are more affluent to undergird the others financially. Large or small donations are always welcome. Further publicity, on the booking form, advertises the "cottages and Scandinavian log cabins, providing holidays for individuals, families and Christian groups", as well as the Granary Barn Centre with office, shop, meeting hall, kitchen and lounge, laundry facilities, ponies, goats, and a games area.

Tom had owned six horses, to provide rides round the field for children. He sold two of the horses, and three goats, to the Jonas Trust; and the other four horses to stables running riding for disabled children. He and Judy found themselves, for the first time in many years, with no more bookings of guests to organise, no more "cooking the breakfasts, etc.", to which Tom referred in the television programme — they had taken in bed-and-breakfast visitors in Elm House over a ten-year period, as well as all the self-catering guests in the lodges and cottages. In 1996 all the bookings were sold, as an ongoing business, to the Jonas Trust. Tom and Judy were very happy with the vision that George, Jill, Peter and Jennie had committed themselves to. Tom undertook to give the Jonas Trust five years to buy Elm House itself and the rest of the estate; not to sell to anyone else in the meantime; and the members of the Trust agreed that if they wished to purchase at any time during that period, they would give twelve months' notice to Tom. All six were willing to proceed on the basis of this verbal contract. If the agreed time ran out with no change, the situation would, as Judy put it, "be reviewed and prayed for". Incidentally, one area of no change: the Jonas four have kept a Sunday evening service on the estate each week, held in the conference centre. Tom and Judy support it once a month. They also go to the "United Christian Worship" in Leyburn once a month; and to the Hollybush Sunday evening worship once a month. What do they do on the fourth evening? Perhaps they have a rest! Or watch "Songs of Praise"?

George Lihou organising pony rides.

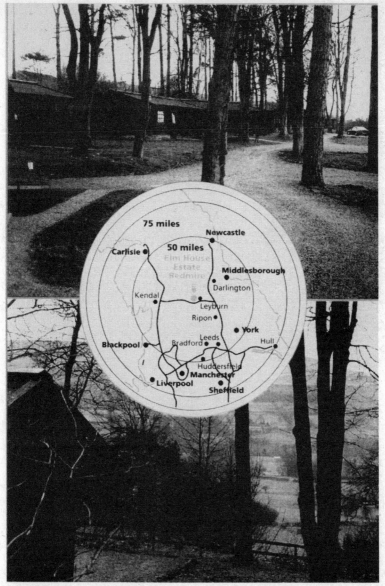

From the brochure issued by the Jonas Trust, showing the convenient
position of the Elm House Christian Holiday Centre.

Chapter 16

Back to Bavaria

When you retire, you have time to think. And as people grow older, they begin to think more about their own past, partly because there is more of it to think about. They begin to study the family tree, to look for missing pieces in the jig-saw of previous generations, to think of all the questions they could have asked their grandparents, if only they had been interested enough. But for some, there has never been an opportunity to ask parents or grandparents. For Tom Walters, the memory of his early childhood days was a blank. Snippets of information about his mother's background and tragic end had come from his Aunt Hanna and, after her death, from correspondence with Susan Koenigsberg in America. Of his father's background he knew nothing. Then the research carried out by Regine Wosnitza for Tyne Tees Television had brought more information than he could ever have expected. He had been to Berlin. He had seen the house where he was born. He had visited the railway station from which his mother was deported; and he had in his possession a document bearing her signature, written a day or two before the deportation.

The television programme had called him "the Boy from Berlin", and it was indeed near Berlin (at Altlandsberg) that he was born. But his mother, who had indeed spent her own childhood in Berlin, had lived for

years, with her father and sister, in Bavaria, until shortly
before her little boy was born. Might it not be possible to
go to Bavaria and visit the family home? That had not been
part of the visit he had made with the television company.
Perhaps there would still be someone living in the area
who remembered his mother — or would it be too late?
And then, for a practical man like Tom, was there any
possibility of compensation, for the loss of a 2,000-acre
estate at Kurzenhof? For many months now the media
(notably BBC Radio 4, The Times newspaper and Time
magazine) had been accumulating evidence of the vast
scale of the plundering of Jewish assets by the Nazis, both
during and after the war, to the profit of some of
Germany's best-known firms, the famous museums of
Paris, the government of Sweden and the Bank of Portugal,
and, overwhelmingly, the banks of Switzerland. Political
and financial leaders had responded to increasing pressure
to investigate, and consider claims for compensation. For
example, on the 4th February 1997, Radio 4 "News at
One" announced that three of the largest banks of
Switzerland had set up a fund of £43 million to help
Holocaust victims. This was corroborated the same
evening by the French television (TF1), which gave the sum
as 100 million Swiss francs, or 400 million French francs.
Finally, in July 1997, the Swiss Bankers' Association
dropped its policy of secrecy and published in The Times
and other leading newspapers world-wide a list of over
two thousand names of "dormant" bank accounts from
the World War II era. Claimants are asked to fill in a
simple form. "No fees are involved. Please come forward.
You will receive prompt and serious attention". For the
vast majority of holocaust victims, it was too late to talk
of compensation. Not only their gold and possessions, but
their very lives, had been stolen from them. Holocaust
survivor groups welcomed the Swiss banks' decision to

publish, but deplored the fifty-year delay.

There is no evidence that the Baumann family had any contact with Swiss banks, although there are two Baumann accounts in the list. What few possessions Eva still had in 1942 were stolen — confiscated — by the Nazis; their value was irrelevant since they also took away her life. Hanna, determined to save herself from Nazi tyranny, fled the country and was forced to sell her property in haste at a very low price. Tom knew that at times she had tried to claim compensation, and wondered whether this was still possible. But in any case he felt he must try to visit the place where the two sisters had lived.

At the end of 1994 Tom sent a video recording of "The Boy from Berlin" to Susan Koenigsberg, Hanna's "foster daughter", now living in California. In Susan's reply, she raises questions about the "perjury" case against Tom's mother, asking: "If the records exist, can you discover whether it was a civil or a criminal complaint? If a civil complaint, were the persons who brought it related to your father?" Susan also talks of a lecture she has attended, by Rabbi Bernard Zlotowitz, commemorating the fiftieth anniversary of the end of the holocaust. He in turn told "the unbelievable story of the only rabbi (Martin Riesenburger) who practised in Berlin throughout the war years (1939-1945) with the knowledge and approval of the Gestapo. Few people even know of his existence and fewer still of his activities. It is thought that he acted under protection: he held services, observed the Jewish holidays, officiated at funerals, even built a Sukkah — all during the time that other Jews were being deported to the concentration camps." In writing about Rabbi Zlotowitz's lecture, Susan quotes him as saying that on May 8th 1995 some Gestapo files were going to be opened. She continues: "Why they were allowed to wait fifty years is not quite clear! Anyway, if you are still in touch with that nice journalist lady who appeared in your film, tell her to check on this, because there may be new details coming out".

Susan's last suggestion fitted in with Tom's own thoughts. If there was one person who could ferret out details from legal archives and make contact with people associated with his childhood days in Germany, it would be "that nice journalist lady". So at the beginning of 1997 he contacted Regine in Berlin by telephone and by letter, and was very pleased when she agreed to help. With power of attorney received from Tom, she would send a request to the court in Füssen to find out more about the Kurzenhof house. She would then go to Füssen and Lechbruck (the nearest village to the Kurzenhof estate) and spend two days looking at documents and making contact with the present owners of the estate, with a view to a possible visit by Tom and Judy.

All this went according to plan. Regine travelled to Lechbruck and booked in at a guesthouse, where the proprietor's son knew where Kurzenhof was. He also knew the name of Fichtel, the grandfather of the present owner, who had apparently at one time bought some land from Eva Baumann. The present owners were named Echtler. Regine decided to check the records at the town hall. There she learned that a certain Hans Hardt had bought Kurzenhof from Hanna and Eva Baumann in 1933. She further discovered that long before the Baumanns had lived there, the Kurzenhof estate was divided into two, and a second farmhouse built. The Echtler family had inherited the original farmhouse and estate, whereas it was "Kurzenhof 2", next door, that Hanna and Eva sold to Hans Hardt, who lived there for some years, after which the property was sold to a hydro-electric company (the Bayerische Wasserkraftwerke) based in Munich. It was an ideal spot for hydro-electric development, because of the fast-flowing River Lech close by. However, the company decided in 1965 to build a large dam for their project, for which they needed some land further down the river, which belonged to the community. They therefore agreed to an exchange: they acquired the land and the community gained Kurzenhof, which however was neglected for nearly thirty years, until the present owner bought it in 1993.

Armed with this information, Regine hired a bicycle to take her the five or six kilometres from Lechbruck to Kurzenhof. She received a friendly welcome from Frau Echtler and her daughter, but they were not able to answer Regine's questions. They kindly telephoned an elderly uncle, who remembered the name Baumann, but with no details. Unfortunately, all the other elderly people on the surrounding farms had died within the past five years. The owner of Kurzenhof 2 was abroad, but Regine was able to walk round and see that the old farm building was still empty and neglected, though the structure was solid. By contrast, the adjoining barn had been pulled down and replaced by a brand new modern house.

Feeling exhilarated both by the beauty of the whole area and by the discoveries made so far, Regine decided to return to the registry office at Füssen. From the records she learned that Hans Hardt, the purchaser of Kurzenhof, had a sister Margarete, whose husband was a university professor named Brühl. Could he be one of the Brühls of Berlin who were related by marriage to the Baumanns and Treumanns? If so, he was probably Jewish, although his brother-in-law Hardt was not. Further investigation revealed that Hardt had offered to buy Kurzenhof for a sum of 22,000 Goldmarks; seven thousand deposit and other expenses to be paid by October 1st 1933, and the remaining 15,000 in mortgage repayments over several years. There were evidently complications, not to say disagreements, between Hans Hardt, his sister Margarete, the Baumann sisters, and Martin Fichtel (the owner of the other Kurzenhof farm, who apparently gave money to Eva at one stage). By June 1939 (the very month that Eva's son Thomas travelled to England), the mortgage was transferred to the name of Margarete Brühl, who took over the responsibility for payments. Hans Hardt apparently remained the legal owner, but in any case his sister Margarete and his wife Ruth Hardt were the legal owners when he died in 1963. At the end of that year, they sold Kurzenhof to the electricity board.

If there was one thing clear from all these revelations, it was that there were further mysteries still to be solved. But first of all, Tom and Judy were to come and see Kurzenhof for themselves. On the 16th June 1997, they flew from Newcastle to Munich (via Brussels), where Regine met them at the airport and where they had arranged to hire a car. Tom had never before driven on the "other" side of the road, nor driven a left-hand-drive car, but with Regine at his side as expert navigator, he accepted the challenge. They negotiated the outskirts of Munich and headed south through the Allgäu district to the Wiesbauer Hotel at Füssen. Almost immediately, they were struck by the natural beauty of the region: rivers and lakes, hills and forests, green pastures with their distinctive herds of cattle (*Allgäu braun Vieh* — surely the prettiest cows you ever saw, thought Judy) and in the distance, but coming nearer as they drove, the majestic mountains that marked the border with Austria.

They quickly settled into the comfortable hotel on the south side of the town of Füssen. As they surveyed the countryside, with fields stretching to the Bavarian Alps, and breathed the freshness of the air, they could understand why Ludwig Bowman had chosen it as a place to retire. Next day they set off to visit Kurzenhof and to meet Wilhelm and Marianne Echtler, the owners of the original farm. On arrival, they saw the two sets of buildings, recognising the old farmhouse from the old photograph they already had and which had been used in the television programme. They chatted to one of the owners of the new house at Kurzenhof 2, and also Marianne Echtler at Kurzenhof 1, who was happy to meet Tom and Judy and be photographed with them; and interested to know that Tom was the son of a previous owner of the other farm. Unknown to Tom and Judy, at this stage, Regine had another interest as well, with a number of questions on sensitive issues. Frau Echtler was happy to tell what she could about the recent history of Kurzenhof, but was surprised to be asked in what year her grandfather, Martin Fichtel, was born. But she gave the answer: 1883. Regine did a quick calculation: he would have been nearly fifty years old in 1931. For she had made her most startling discovery yet during her recent research, namely, that Tom's father was probably none other than Marianne Echtel's grandfather, Martin Fichtel, Eva's next-door neighbour! It was obvious that Marianne had no knowledge of this period of her grandfather's life, and certainly no idea that she might be related to Tom. Regine decided that this was not the right time to tell her. She returned with Tom and Judy to the hotel and that evening carefully explained that she thought she had found Tom's father.

How had Regine made this identification? By thinking about the court case, when Eva had been given a prison sentence for perjury. It must have been reported in the newspapers, she thought. So she wrote to the archives at Kempten, the district town in Bavaria where the court was held, and soon received a photocopy of a lengthy article that appeared in the *Allgäuer Tagblatt* (daily newspaper) on February 7th 1936. The first surprise was that this was the second court case that Eva had been involved in. She had already filed a claim for maintenance in 1934. She had stated that the father of her child Thomas was Martin

Fichtel. She had won the case. The County Court at Füssen upheld her claim and ordered Fichtel to pay alimony of RM35 per month, a sum which would more than double her income — as late as 1941, at the old people's home in Schoenhauser Allee, she earned a net salary of RM27. In the autumn of 1931, when the intercourse took place, her father had just died and she was often alone in the house. Martin Fichtel apparently had a serious hip injury from the First World War — his granddaughter remembers him as not being able to walk without crutches; so it is likely that he too would often be alone, while his wife and two sons were at work or school. In 1931 he would be forty-eight and Eva twenty-seven. However, in 1934, he was not prepared to accept the court's order without a fight. His appeal was turned down by the district court in Kempten on June 1st 1934, but in January 1935 he tried again, claiming that he had new evidence. He had found a policeman and a doctor to testify to Eva's immoral reputation; and a further witness, Max Beller, who declared that he also had had sexual relations with her. Fichtel evidently did not deny his intimacy, but simply argued that since he was not the only one, Eva had lied when she said, on oath, that she was certain who her child's father was. This time the court, in its decision taken on the 6th February 1936, accepted his story, released him from the payments, and found Eva guilty of perjury, with a sentence of one year and four months in prison, loss of civil rights for three years and permanent incapacity to act as a witness in any legal proceedings. There was an attempt in the court to bring evidence from a Berlin doctor that Eva was mentally deficient, with a "moral mental deficiency", but the prosecutor declared that he considered the defendant to be of sound mind.

One strange aspect of this whole affair is that nowhere in the record files or in the *Allgäuer Tagblatt* article is there any mention that Eva was Jewish, unless the judge's statement that "she was certainly able to understand the importance the German people attach to the meaning of an oath" is a veiled way of indicating that she was Jewish, without actually saying so. This would enable the Nazi court to present an image of efficient impartiality, although in fact by this time there were already laws against "non-Aryans" which meant that any semblance of impartiality was fast disappearing down the slippery slope of racist discrimination.

After the disclosure of all this information about his mother's trial, Tom was all the more painfully aware of how much his mother must have suffered in those 1930s years, as she struggled to assure his survival, as well as her own. Then someone suggested that it would take their enquiries a step further if they could visit the cemetery at Lechbruck, to see if Martin Fichtel was buried there, since they now knew his year of birth. This they did the next morning and soon found his grave, with a brand new headstone. There were five people buried there: Martin Fichtel and his wife, both born in 1883 and both having died in 1967; their son Dominikus, who was evidently killed during the war; and their younger son and his wife, who were the parents of Marianne. It was a moving moment for Tom to think that this might be the tomb of the father whose identity he had thought was lost for ever.

The rest of that day was spent seeing some of the sights of Bavaria, notably the fantastic castle at Neuschwanstein, one of many built by Ludwig II, who was king of Bavaria from 1864 (at the age of eighteen). Eccentric and unpredictable, he met and befriended the composer Richard Wagner in 1864 and sponsored the Wagner concerts at Bayreuth, the first of which was performed in his presence in 1876. He was known as Mad King Ludwig and, at his mysterious death by drowning in 1886, was succeeded by his brother Otto, who also was mentally unbalanced. What an unstable world of fantasy the government of Bavaria was in those days! No wonder the monarchy came to an end in the growing unrest of the twentieth century!

On the third day of Tom and Judy's visit, they went to Ulm and Herrlingen, the place where Tom had spent a year shortly before being taken to England. Wisely, they decided to have a rest from driving and take the train. They were met at Herrlingen station by a gracious lady, Frau Dr Warthinger, whom Regine had located and who was able to give a conducted tour of the Waldheim home where children found shelter in the 1930s; with its surrounding woodland area, including the impressive house and grounds where Field Marshal Rommel lived, until ordered to commit suicide by Hitler in 1944, because of his links with the group involved in a failed assassination plot. We may wonder if Tom ever caught a glimpse of Rommel in his days of success and prestige! At the beginning of the 1930s, there was a large house called "Waldheim"at Herrlingen, whose owner, Käthe Hamburg, took in orphaned children or children without a home. Käthe was helped by a young woman named Elsa. One day a young man named Ernst Franzen turned up. He was a craftsman, an apprentice, and in those days in Germany apprentices used to travel through the country, to work in different parts of the country and gather experience. So Ernst came to Herrlingen, fell in love with Elsa and married her. Then they both helped Käthe with the home, as volunteers, without a proper salary, just personal expenses. Another helper in the home was Käthe's sister, Ruth, who worked as a teacher and was also remembered as an accomplished violinist. The grounds of the house were extensive, with plenty of room to build a second house; which is just what Käthe did, as a home for Ernst and Elsa Franzen, in appreciation of all the help they had given. The Franzens were now able to take in children themselves. In the mid 1930s, Käthe had seven foster children who lived with her all the time, as well as many others who came to stay during the school holidays. The Franzens' home served as an annexe for younger children.

Two of the children in Käthe Hamburg's home were Gretel and Hans Fichtner, twins, born in 1922. Tom and Judy were excited to hear that Regine had made arrangements for them to go and meet Hans, who still lived not far away, in Ulm, with his daughter Ruth. His sister Gretel now lived in Berlin. Ruth now gave the visitors a warm welcome. They learned that she had done a lot of research on the children's home and had published a thesis on the subject in 1986. Hans soon joined them. He seemed tired and reserved at first, but soon grew animated as he described, with obvious affection, the foster home where he had grown up (after he and his sister had been abandoned by their natural parents). He didn't remember Tom, who was ten years younger and in the other household, but a warm friendship developed as they talked of their common experience (even if Tom couldn't remember his!). Ruth found, among the photographs in her collection, an exact copy of one that Tom had inherited from Hanna; and two others, one of which had the names of the children on the back: Karin (the Franzens' own daughter), Bruno, Erika, Ernst-Otto, and Thomas! It was a moving experience for Tom to see himself in the surroundings of those chaotic days, with the loving care of foster parents providing a haven of peace amid the raging storm of persecution. But he had no recollection of the home, no recognition of any aspect of the surrounding parkland. His memory was a blank. The turmoil and upheaval of the next couple of years had wiped the slate clean.

Regine kept in touch with the people visited, after she returned to Berlin, and Tom and Judy to England. She also researched and clarified details of Hanna's compensation claims. Hanna had stored much of the contents of the Kurzenhof home (twenty-nine boxes, cases, chests, porcelain, glassware, bedding, skis, as well as small items of furniture and thirty paintings, some of them valuable) with a removal firm, Weissenhorn & Co., in Augsburg, on the 21st October 1933, before emigrating to England. The rest of her furniture she had sold at throwaway prices. She had insured the goods stored with the removal firm for RM15,000. It was 1953 before she was able to return. Only fourteen of the twenty-nine boxes remained. A law had been passed by the Nazi government, decreeing that the property of Jews who had emigrated became the property of the German Reich. However, all the evidence was that the missing boxes had been looted after the fall of that government at the end of the war, so that the tax authorities were still arguing in 1960 (in answer to Hanna's lawyer, A.L. Oppenheim) that they were not liable for restitution, unless it could be proved that the German Reich had actually implemented the 1941 law in respect of these items, and taken possession of them. The wrangle continued. Oppenheim was able to find out that the money in Hanna's bank accounts had been confiscated, and also the contents of a suitcase deposited with the Commerzbank in Munich. He also pointed out the absurdity of any suggestion that she, being Jewish, could have returned to claim any property during the war years. Eventually, on the 3rd July 1961, the Highest District Court in Munich agreed to a compensation of DM5,000.

Regine also had some more information relating to the sale of the Kurzenhof 2 estate. In 1949 Hanna's claims for compensation against Hardt were reinforced in a letter written by a lawyer, Ludwig Burghardt, writing on her behalf. He emphasised that Hardt and his sister (Margarete Brühl) had knowingly exploited the situation in which Hanna and Eva Baumann found themselves in 1933: the need to sell very quickly. He declared that instead of the sum of RM22,000 paid (or rather, promised to be paid) by Hardt, the real value of the estate was RM35,000, which was the price that Ludwig Bowman had paid for it in the late twenties. By contrast, Hardt found a witness in the Baumanns' neighbour, Martin Fichtel, to assert that Kurzenhof was not worth more than RM22,000 at the time it was sold to Hardt. Burghardt, in his letter, requests that Fichtel's testimony be rejected on the grounds of his probable animosity towards Ms Bowman because of a former legal dispute over her sister's maintenance claim against him (that is to say, the dispute as to whether or not he was the father of her child Thomas). In the same letter, Burghardt refers to the two sisters as Professor Brühl's nieces. He also refers, not without scepticism, to a suggestion that Brühl had really wanted to buy Kurzenhof for himself (could he have thought that, although Jewish, he and his property would be safe because his wife was not Jewish?) and had persuaded his wife and her brother (Margarete and Hans Hardt) to buy it in their name. Whatever the truth was of purchase and proxy, of exploitation and intrigue, Hans Hardt and Hanna Bowman agreed to an out-of-court settlement, at the Schwaben Compensation Office in Augsburg on February 20th 1950. Hardt was to pay DM5,000 into an account named by Hanna, in mortgage instalments starting on the 1st April 1950. All demands of both parties were thereby wiped out. The settlement applied also to Eva Baumann's heirs. At this time Tom, busy with his apprenticeship in England, was seventeen years old, not in close touch with Hanna, and would know nothing of these negotiations, or even of the existence of Kurzenhof.

To conclude the story of the Bavarian visit: Regine wrote to both Marianne Echtler at Kurzenhof and Hans Fichtner and his daughter Ruth at Ulm. In her letter to Marianne, she broke the news that we thought her grandfather, Martin Fichtel, was Tom's father. It was a complete revelation to her. She had never heard any inkling of the story and was shocked to hear it, as Regine found out when she followed up the letter with a telephone call. Regine reassured Marianne that there was no question of accusing her of anything. She was also thankful that Marianne remained friendly and understanding, as she thanked Regine for the photograph of herself (Marianne) with Tom and Judy, whilst at the same time being honest enough to say that she could not say thankyou for the other photographs (of Tom's mother and aunt and grandfather). Nor, if she thought of it, did she offer to send a photograph of her grandfather, which Tom would very much like to have seen. However, some weeks later, good news! After further communication with Regine, she agreed to send a photograph of her grandfather — surely a token of understanding between Regine and Marianne which is a tribute to them both.

Regine's letter to the Fichtners at Ulm accompanied a video recording of the Tyne Tees television programme, "The Boy from Berlin". In reply they sent their warmest regards, saying that they liked the video very much and had already made two copies for the archives they are keeping of all the "Waldheimers" — the children of the Waldheim home at Herrlingen.

Regine Wosnitza with Tom and
Judy at Kurzenhof.

Judy and Tom with Marianne
Echtler (his niece?) at Kurzenhof.

The mountains on the border of Bavaria and Austria, which Ludwig
Bowman and his daughters would see every day.

Kurzenhof 2 farm, in
Ludwig Bowman's day.

Kurzenhof 2 farm, new and old
(photo 17th June 1997).

The headstone of Martin
Fichtel's grave.

Happy birthday, Thomas! Waldheim,
Herrlingen (near Ulm), 5th June 1938.

Aus den Gerichtsfälen

Schwurgericht Kempten

Meineid

Der zweite und letzte Fall der diesjährigen 1. Schwur=
gerichtsperiode am Landgericht Kempten betraf die am 27.
August 1904 in Berlin=Schöneberg geborene ledige Eva
Baumann, zuletzt in Berlin=Schmargendorf, seit 10.
Dezember 1935 in Untersuchungshaft. Der Anklage liegt
folgender Tatbestand zugrunde: Eva Baumann wurde
in Sachen ihres außerehelichen Kindes Thomas Baumann
gegen Martin Fichtel von Kurzenhof, Gemeinde Lechbruck,
wegen Vaterschaft und Unterhalt am 28. Februar 1934 vor
dem Amtsgericht Füssen als Zeugin vernommen und be=
eidigt. Dabei gab sie an, in der einrechnungsfähigen Zeit —
8. August 1931 bis 7. Dezember 1931 — nur mit dem
Bauern Martin Fichtel geschlechtlich verkehrt zu haben. Sie
verschwieg hier bewußt, daß sie an einem Sonntag im Sep=
tember 1931 auch mit dem Bauernsohn Max Beller von
Tiefenbruck intim verkehrt hatte. Auch die Angabe der Be=
schuldigten, den ersten Verkehr mit einem gewissen Jakob
König gehabt zu haben, war bewußt unwahr, weil sie schon
im Juni 1931 mit Fichtel geschlechtlich verkehrt hatte. Auf
Grund dieser unwahren Aussagen wurde Martin Fichtel
durch Urteil des Amtsgerichts Füssen vom 14. März 1934
als Vater des von der Angeschuldigten am 5. Juni 1932 ge=
borenen Kindes Thomas Baumann festgestellt und zur
Zahlung einer monatlichen Unterhaltsrente von 35 Mark
verurteilt. Durch Urteil des Landgerichts Kempten vom
1. Juni 1934 wurde die von Fichtel gegen das amtsgericht=
liche Urteil eingelegte Berufung verworfen.

Report in the *Allgäuer Tagblatt* of Eva's second court case, in 1936.

The Franzens' house, where Thomas lived 1938-9.

Part of the Waldheim family: Thomas (front centre); behind him Käthe Hamburg; on his left Karin Franzen.

The Waldheim house at
Herrlingen.

*Von 1927 bis 1939
lebte in diesem Haus,
dem WALDHEIM,
Käthe Hamburg
mit ihren Pflegekindern.
Sie war Lehrerin
im Landschulheim Herrlingen.*

Plaque recording Käthe Hamburg's
care for homeless children at
Waldheim.

Hans Fichtner, former Waldheim resident, with Tom Walters.

Chapter 17

The contract

If you make a contract, it's nice to have everything "cut and dried" no loose ends, no misunderstandings or mysteries. But Tom and Judy came back from Germany without any prospect of putting right the injustice of imposed financial transactions, without the absolutely certain identification of Tom's father, and with the irrevocable pain of the murder of his mother. Was the trip worth while? And was it the final chapter in the story? The answers to these questions must be yes to the first and no to the second. "Bavaria Revisited" was the appropriate counterbalance for "The Boy from Berlin". To visit Kurzenhof was to be able to picture the home that Eva shared with her sister and father. It was, after all, the place where Tom's life began, even though in circumstances the family would not have chosen. One of the highlights of the tour was the visit to Ulm: seeing the photographs, hearing the memories of the kindness the Waldheim children received from selfless people in difficult and dangerous circumstances. One of Hans Fichtner's memories was even more bitter than Tom's, for whereas Tom's mother had struggled to protect him, sometimes at great risk to herself, Hans had to live with the knowledge that his mother didn't want him.

When Tom was asked if he suffered an identity crisis, he answered: not when he was a child. But now, he knows grief, especially on the church's "mother's day", as he looks back to his early separation from his mother, and feels that he never had the chance to get to know her. It is not surprising that he is essentially a family man. He loves to be with his children and grandchildren, and indeed enjoys company in general. Neither shy nor self-conscious, he is gregarious by instinct and friendly on principle; happy to talk to anyone who will talk to him. "I need people", he says, "I can't exist on my own." Most of all, he is devoted to his wife Judy, and she to him; although on one occasion, when someone had the temerity to ask her if she would approve of his marrying again if she pre-deceased him, she mischievously replied, "Of course, but who would have him?" Tom and Judy's partnership, their working and relaxing and consulting together, and his respect for her advice and spiritual insights, may be illustrated allegorically from his comment one day at the wheel of his car: "I love driving, so long as I know the way. If I don't know the way, then I need Judy."

Judy found inspiration one day in thinking of Robert Browning's poem:

> Grow old along with me!
> The best is yet to be,
> The last of life, for which the first was made:
> Our times are in His hand
> Who saith, "A whole I planned,
> Youth shows but half; trust God, see all, nor be afraid!"

As they look to the future, she and Tom are concerned that their present should be, and should be seen to be, under God's guiding hand. With regard to their time, their energy, their possessions, Tom says: "In fact we owe everything to God. It's only loaned to us; we are stewards". He likes making money and he enjoys giving it away, but he doesn't believe in throwing it away. He and Judy believe in tithing, literally, which means putting aside at least ten per cent of income for God's work. They support many missionary and charity organisations, and have begging letters from many more. They take a particular interest in home-based missions, concerned with evangelism in Britain, including United Christian Broadcasters (UCB); as well as giving support to Christian workers in Russia, Romania and other eastern European countries, to several Jewish organisations and to local churches. They believe God has spoken to them through the words of Loren Cunningham, the founder of Youth with a Mission. This is what he says (in his book, *Daring to Live on the Edge*), first of all quoting from Deuteronomy:

> You may say to yourself, "My power and the strength of my hands have produced this wealth for me." But remember the Lord your God, for it is he who gives you the ability to produce wealth... (Deuteronomy 8:17,18). And... though your riches increase, do not set your heart on them (Psalm 62:10)
>
> Paul told Timothy to tell the entrepreneurs of his day not to become conceited or to fix their hope on the uncertainty of riches, but on God. He also told them to do good, to be rich in good works and generosity (1 Timothy 6:17-19).
>
> All Christians are to be generous and give, but God has given some people special talent to make money so they can give more to God's work. We could call them "Holy Spirit Entrepreneurs". Paul referred to these people as having the gift of helping (1 Corinthians 12:29) or the gift of giving (Romans 12:8). One of the many ways God provides is by giving such people ideas which make money."

Cunningham continues with advice on how to give money away! "Everyone is different when it comes to giving... Some prefer giving to mercy ministries; others want their gift to go to evangelism". To this Tom and Judy would answer that they want to do both, which is why they are giving the highest priority to supporting YWAM, including full financial support to their son Philip, as he shares that organisation's commitment to helping those in need, body and soul, wherever the door of opportunity is open.

For Tom and Judy, it is important to co-operate with Christians in all denominations, particularly in their own local area. They took part in a "march for Jesus" united prayer meeting, held in a local Methodist church in the Spring of 1997; and on August bank holiday the Churches Together committee (Roman Catholic, Church of England and Methodist) organised "the Tent of the Good Shepherd" at the Wensleydale agricultural show, held annually at Leyburn. On the hour, from 11am to 3pm, there was a 10-minute worship service slot; every half past the hour a children's video; also Christian art work and a bookstall, and people on hand to help those who wanted to talk. Tom was responsible for the publicity: posters; writing to church leaders; advertising in the Press. He and Judy are equally glad to co-operate wherever they can with good causes in the village and locality. There are requests to open the gardens once or twice a year for a charity function, with stalls and teas — an activity which is usually shared by a dozen or more other gardens in the village of Redmire. In 1996 it was in support of the Red Cross; in 1997 to raise money for a scanner for Northallerton Hospital. Sometimes the main lounge of Elm House is made available for a political meeting, with local MP William Hague. "Would you have a Labour Party meeting as well?" Tom was asked. With a smile he said, "Oh yes, we'd let them in if they asked". But Tom is careful to distinguish between

Christian commitment and political affiliation. Should everyone be a Christian? "That's a choice. I would try to persuade. It's a life and death difference; more to gain and lose in this question (than in politics)". "From the pulpit, I'd tell everyone I'm a Christian"; but not preach party politics from the pulpit. But we should preach on issues that are related to the homeless and underprivileged. "If we don't shout, who will?" And Tom would preach "against VAT on fuel, against Sunday trading, against sleaze, against a lot of privatisation and against 'obscene' pay and pensions for top directors".

To celebrate their ruby wedding, Tom and Judy decided to invite all the family, about twenty of them. But they didn't stop there. They invited everyone in the Hollybush fellowship and everyone in the parish of Redmire, that is to say, the whole population of Redmire village, about 260 people. Invitation cards were distributed, marked RSVP and "no presents, please". Their wedding day in 1957 was in April, but the 1997 celebration was held on the 28th May. Four hundred guests accepted the invitation. A marquee was specially erected on the lawn, with a buffet supper, a bar, and popular music playing, including the top ten of 1957! There was plenty of food. The view across the fields was beautiful, with a herd of Friesian cows grazing peacefully nearby, in the evening sunshine. After the refreshments, the guests took their seats in the tent for the grand finale of the celebrations. Tom was keen to "sing the Lord's song" in a way that showed the driving force of his life, but with a sensitivity to different people's backgrounds, not forgetting his own, emphasising "what God has done for me", and, because of that, a confidence in the future, if that future is in the hands of God. Three accomplished soloists contributed to the entertainment: Margaret Westwood, from the Methodist chapel at Leyburn; Charles Marwood, a farmer and member of

Hollybush fellowship; and Cynthia Wilkinson, former professional singer and, with her husband, a leader of Hollybush. Four more friends, Bill Field, a churchwarden at Redmire; lay reader Raymond Dawson; Helen Lee, founder of the Leyburn United Christian Worship; and Jim Wilkinson, pastor of Hollybush; all brought their tributes and good wishes to Tom and Judy, commendably observing the five-minute time limit each of them was allowed! The blessing at the end was said by the Revd Albert Atkinson, former vicar of Bolton-cum-Redmire and before that a member of the Salvation Army! (The present vicar, Susan Whitehouse, was unable to be present.) There was also community hymn-singing. Tom had chosen hymns known and loved across the denominations and, characteristically, each one expressing faith in the future: Amazing Grace, Blessed Assurance, How Great Thou Art, Abide with me, When the roll is called up yonder, When the saints go marching in and O that will be glory for me.

Before the blessing was said and the informal celebration and music continued until midnight, Tom made his own speech. He thanked everyone for helping to make a memorable evening. He offered the use, free of charge, of the marquee, for a wedding reception, to anyone who could arrange it before the end of that week, and with a benevolent but mischievous look in his eye, looked pointedly at a blushing young couple on the front row. (The offer was not taken up!) Then he recalled Judy's reference to the words, "The best is yet to be", and continued:

I wondered what she meant. Was it that we were soon to travel to Germany to trace the estate which had once been owned by my family — for which I still have the Contract?

My mother, who was Jewish and her sister, my aunt, were left the 2,000 acre estate on the death of their father in 1931. In 1933 Hitler came to power and he decreed that nobody should trade with Jews, so my family had to mortgage the property and borrow money in order to survive, but they soon realised they would have to leave the estate, so found someone willing to take over the mortgage, but he soon defaulted on the payments. So did "the best is yet to come" mean that I would reclaim my German inheritance or did it mean that it would be the place we would move to after Elm House?

We first saw Elm House in 1984, on a grey, misty September day and did not initially think it was for us, but, after a few days' prayer and thought, we changed our minds and realised that God was leading us to buy Elm House Estate. We made an offer which was accepted and in due course signed the Contract which committed us to pay for the estate.

What a wonderful home we have, and what marvellous views — could anything be better than this?

But one day we shall move and then another Contract will be drawn up, with conditions and the price to be agreed and then we shall sign the Contract, but I think I know the answer because Judy and I know that a property is being prepared for us and it will be better than the German property or Elm House. We have seen the Contract and have signed it, which means we have committed ourselves to a binding agreement.

There are two wonderful things about this Contract: 1) It is available to everyone, not just us; and 2) The price for the property has already been paid in full; there is nothing else to pay. It's a long contract; there are some things I do not fully understand, but there are also many assurances.

Tom reinforced the theme of confidence with Bible quotations:

For God so loved the world that he gave his only begotten Son, that whoever believes in him shall not perish but have eternal life. (John 3:16)

He has made everything beautiful in its time. He also has planted eternity in men's hearts and minds. (Ecclesiastes 3:11)

Do not let your hearts be troubled. Trust in God; trust also in me. In my Father's house are many rooms; if it were not so, I would have told you. I am going there to prepare a place for you. And if I go and prepare a place for you, I will come back and take you to be with me, that you also may be where I am. You know the way to the place where I am going.

Thomas said to him, "Lord, we do not know where you are going, so how can we know the way?"

Jesus answered, "I am the Way and the Truth and the Life. No one comes to the Father except through me. If you really knew me, you would know my Father as well. From now on you do know him and have seen him". (John 14:1-7)

Some weeks later, Tom put his thoughts into print, and added a final paragraph:

We have now returned from our trip to Germany and yes we found the family estate. It has changed hands several times and the land has been sold, so no I won't be able to claim my inheritance, but this doesn't worry me at all because my heavenly inheritance will never be lost and I agree with Judy that "the best is yet to come".

So Tom builds his faith and life on "many assurances" contained in a divine contract, in spite of the things that are hard to understand.

One of the controversies recently aired in the Press is whether Britain could have done more to stop the holocaust. "One of the best things Britain ever did", says Paul Johnson, writing in the *Daily Mail*, February 27th 1997, "was to welcome Jewish refugees fleeing Continental persecution. We have been, and still are being, richly rewarded for our toleration and foresight". The same newspaper, three months later, has an article by Tom Bower (May 20th 1997), in which he declares that as early as 1940 the British Foreign Office had precise details of the holocaust and knew, in 1942, that Hitler had approved the "Final Solution". According to Bower, British intelligence was expert in decoding Germany's top secret messages; an advantage that enabled the Allies to bring an end to the U-boat menace in the Atlantic and defeat Rommel in North Africa. Why, he argues, could not the RAF have bombed Auschwitz or the railways leading to it, which would have saved at least the Hungarian Jews? He blames the government, and particularly Foreign Secretary Anthony Eden, for preferring not to believe the ample evidence of genocide. Bower's damning indictment, however, is challenged in yet another article (July 5th 1997) by a professor of modern history in the University of Wales, William Rubinstein, who is himself a Jew who lost relatives in the concentration camps, but points out that before the war Hitler's policy was expulsion of Jews from Germany, not extermination, that over 70% of Germany's Jews managed to leave the country, with more in 1939 (the year of Tom Walters' escape) than in any other year. Once the war started, says Rubinstein, Britain simply did not have the means to end the slaughter, other than by winning the war. In the meantime, a National Committee for Rescue from Nazi Terror was founded by Eleanor Rathbone and Victor Gollancz. Its members included leading politicians, archbishops and other people of influence in church and state.

A postscript to the larger controversy of Britain's attitude to victims of the holocaust was highlighted in Granada Television's "World in Action" programme on the 8th September 1997. Many families deposited their money in Britain before the war, hoping to use it to start a new life when the horrors of Nazi persecution were over. Understandably, these bank accounts, from customers in enemy countries (some two thousand of them), were frozen during the war. What has recently come to light, with new access to hitherto secret documents, is that these deposits were confiscated, after the war. They were dealt with by the "trading with the enemy" department. It is not known how many of them belonged to Jews, but evidently little attempt was made to distinguish between "enemies" and "victims". Some survivors and relatives have been trying to retrieve their assets for fifty years. The British government and banks have at last promised an investigation.

Another question mark for many people lies over the future of Israel. Tom shares his son Philip's view that God has a special plan for the people he chose three and a half millennia ago. They would both endorse the view expressed in the following declaration:

Israel. The Holy Land. There is no area of the world like it. Its language is a modern miracle. Its past is pivotal in understanding world history. Its chief city has a special role to play in international events. But more important than all of this — and the key to a

proper understanding of Israel's place in world events — is its Messiah: the Saviour of the world. For while much of Israel has rejected him, he has not rejected them, but intends to bring about their renewal and restoration before the close of the age.
(Lance Lambert: *The Uniqueness of Israel*)

A more sombre note is struck by William Rees-Mogg's article, "The Unpromising Land of Zion" in *The Times* (August 14th, 1997). Starting with Herzl's belief, a hundred years ago, that Jews would never be safe except in their own country, he explains that many liberal Jewish intellectuals took an opposite view, believing that it made more sense for Jews to be assimilated into all the nations of Europe, and beyond. It was only the holocaust that convinced them that Herzl was right. Now Rees-Mogg examines the precarious security of Israel and asks the question: "If assimilation cannot protect Jews, does it follow that the nation state can do so?" and gives his own answer, "...only if it can win peace with its neighbours".

Tom Walters' testimony poses another provocative question: can anyone be both a Jew and a Christian? David Stern, in his book, *Messianic Jewish Manifesto*, affirms that "Jewish Christian" is a contradiction in terms. Stern is right, of course, in saying that the term "Christian" was invented by Gentiles, but he is surely wrong in saying that it was applied only to Gentiles. In Antioch, where the name was coined, the church (that is to say, the group of people who accepted Jesus as Messiah, or Christ) comprised both Jews and Gentiles. When Helen Shapiro accepted Jesus as the Jewish Messiah and Lord of her life, she was astonished when someone joyfully said to her, "Now you are a Christian!" (see her book, *Walking back to happiness*.) She soon realised this was true, but never ceased to regard herself as Jewish. So also Michele

Guinness, author of *Made for each other*, sees Christianity as a fulfilment of Judaism, but thinks the church should learn more from its Jewish roots, particularly in seeing life as a whole, not divided between the sacred and the secular. Tom has said that he is proud to be a Jew and proud to be a Christian. He accepts that he is German. He is grateful for being brought to England and naturalised English. He is profoundly thankful that the Nazis were crushed. He is not a pacifist: "I would fight for my country" (that is, for Britain). We might ask if it is possible to be "proud" of our birth, since we did nothing to bring it about; or whether being a Christian (that is, accepting Jesus as a saviour from sin) is incompatible with being proud. But no doubt Tom, in using these words, is really saying, with the apostle Paul, "I am not ashamed of the gospel of Christ".

There remains the question of justice, for Hitler and the others who shared in his crimes against humanity. In his teen-age years, Tom admired David Ross's preaching, which at times included fierce warnings about hell, to shake people out of their complacency. But Hitler was not complacent; he was energetically and consistently sadistic. Is he in hell? And if so, is it because he was extraordinarily evil, or because he failed to repent? While some Christians would unhesitatingly preach the damnation of hell, others are disturbed by the thought of a kind of divine Auschwitz, all the more dreadful because it is eternal. Can it in any sense be said of the holocaust that "God meant it for good"? These are the words that Joseph said to his brothers, who had sold him into slavery in Egypt. They are often quoted to make the point that good can come out of evil. God had overruled the brothers' evil action and used Joseph to save Egypt, and his own family, from starvation. But it is difficult to see any beneficial outcome that could justify the horror of the holocaust, even if it is true that it led to the creation of the State of Israel.

Tom and Judy wisely leave these unanswerable questions to the wisdom and justice of God. They believe that "the Judge of all the earth" will do right. It may be appropriate to quote the words of Ludwig Wittgenstein, born, like Hitler, in Austria, and in the same week; later naturalised British and during the second world war professor of philosophy at Cambridge. He wrote:

> *An Gott glauben heißt sehen,*
> *daß es mit den Tatsachen der Welt*
> *noch nicht abgetan ist.*

> (To believe in God is to see
> that with the pattern of world events
> all is not yet finished.)

Tom places himself firmly within that pattern, in the words he spoke on Tyne Tees Television:

> As far as becoming a Christian... I don't know what my mother would have thought of it, because she was a Jewess, and she might have thought this was a bit difficult; but if she could see now, where I am and what's happened to me, I'm sure she would have said, "Thank God!"

Judy and Tom in retirement!

The marquee specially pitched for ruby wedding celebrations.

Judy and Tom welcoming guests.

Tom has the last word.

At the entrance to Elm House: advertising for the 1997 general election.

Photo taken at Kurzenhof in 1959: Martin Fichtel with two neighbours and, on his left, his twelve-year-old granddaughter Marianne (who sent the photo to Tom and Judy with her best wishes, in 1997).

Postscript

I should also like to add my comments to the book *The Boy From Berlin*. In the first place, I was asked, in a letter from Ray and Barbara Belfield in 1996, to write a book; also the same year we had a letter from Jim Ross, to write a book. This seemed to be God saying, "Put it all down on paper!" The TV Programme, "The Boy from Berlin", made a big impact, not only on me, but on a lot of people. It was seen by over a million people on Tyne Tees and Yorkshire television, and after three years I am still asked to go and speak about the programme, with two more talks before the end of this year and another next year.

As a result of the letters, it was suggested that we ask and meet Bob Burt, who knew me soon after I first came over from Germany, but whom we had not seen for over forty years. A contact was made: we met and, as they say, hit it off. Over a period of time we met and talked in each other's homes, and also recorded, until Bob had seen all my papers. This also resulted in our asking Regine Wosnitza (from Berlin) to press on and find out the missing pieces, as it were.

Bob Burt said that he would write the story for me. Over the year October 1996 to October 1997, we have made contact on many occasions and also been to Germany together.

On Friday, 3rd October 1997, Judy and I called at Bob's house, had a meal and were given the finished book, which we brought home. Regine came from Germany on the 5th October and returned on the 9th October; while here she too read the book. After she left, Judy read it and it was taken to Hollybush for Jim Wilkinson to read and comment. I collected it on Sunday, 26th October and by the 29th had read it.

I would like to thank Regine Wosnitza for all the research she has undertaken and all that she has found out over the last three years, as we have got to know each other and she has become a friend. I would also like to say thank you to Bob Burt for putting up with me and trying to get me to think of the past (though sometimes I couldn't help him much); undertaking to write such a wonderful book, with all the information available to him and all the background books to be read. He has become a great friend and has done the impossible.

I would also like to thank Judy for being so helpful and considerate, for the TV programme and book have taken over three years of our life; also the family and so many friends, including Mark Robinson (producer of the TV programme), all the TV crew, the people at Hollybush and the pastor for letting us film there.

May I say, the past affects the present, and the present the future. "God holds the key of all unknown, and I am glad". None of this in my life would have happened if God had not been there from the beginning. The Bible says he knew us before the foundation of the world. If you have read the book, I want to tell you that God loves you and wants you to know him as I know him. How can this happen? By putting our faith in him and believing that he is God over all. The past can be forgiven, because Jesus died for us on the cross, to save us, to make us a people for the present, to serve him and share our faith; and the future is to know God and have eternal life. The rest is history, as you have read in the book.

Tom
29th October 1997

Tom Walters: an identity crisis?
(Photo by Tony Bartholomew, *Northern Echo*, November 14th 1994.)

Bibliography

Birkenhead News and *Bebington News* (contemporary articles in Birkenhead and Bebington Reference Libraries)
Philippe Boegner: *Ici on a aimé les Juifs* (Éditions J-C Lattès, 1982)
A.H. Boulton: *Full Forty Years* (1967)
E.H. Broadbent: *The Pilgrim Church* (Pickering & Inglis, 1931)
Michael Brown: *Our Hands are Stained with Blood* (Destiny Image Publishers, PA, USA, 1992)
W.S. Churchill: *My Early Life* (The Reprint Society, London; originally Macmillan, 1930)
F.R. Coad: *A History of the Brethren Movement* (Paternoster, 1968)
Dan Cohn-Sherbok: *The Crucified Jew* (Fount, 1992)
Loren Cunningham: *Daring to Live on the Edge* (Hodder & Stoughton, 1991)
B. Edwards: *The Rise of the USA* (Blackie, 1968)
Martin Gilbert: *Holocaust Maps and Photographs, a visual narrative,* Fifth (Holocaust Educational Trust) Edition, London, 1998.
Hill, Fenwick, Forbes & Noakes: *Blessing the Church?* (Eagle, 1995)
Thomas Keneally: *Schindler's Ark* (Hodder & Stoughton, 1989)
Lance Lambert: *The Uniqueness of Israel* (Kingsway, 1995)
Mark Laurie: *Dissertation on the Holocaust* (1995)
Herbert Levy: *Voices from the Past* (Temple House books, 1995)
Isabelle McGregor: *Redmire, a patchwork of its history* (1989)
The Northern Echo, November 14th 1994
David Porter: *The Vienna Passage* (Eagle, 1995).
Gerald Reitlinger: *The Final Solution* (Vallentine, Mitchell, 1968)
Ian Schott: *The Life and Times of Hitler* (Paragon Books, 1994)

Sélection du Reader's Digest: *Wallenberg* (May 1991), *Schindler* (November 1994).

David Stern: *Messianic Jewish Manifesto* (Jewish New Testament Publications, 1988)

Corrie Ten Boom: *The Hiding Place* (Hodder & Stoughton, 1971)

C. Warren & J. Benson: *Thetis, "The Admiralty Regrets", the disaster in Liverpool Bay* (Avid Publications, 1997)

Jim Wilkinson & Chris Spencer: *Miracle Valley* (Marshall Pickering, 1984)

Yad Vashem, Jerusalem (official guide)